ACCOLADES

"...and into plowshares turn their swords...
Nations shall learn war no more."
Isaiah 2:4

'Cross the Pond

Dedicated to Our Fellow Appalachians
Who Never Returned to the Mountains.

Compiled and edited by Wess Harrris

'Cross the Pond

Appalachian Community Services
229 Birtrice Road
Gay, West Virginia 25244

Cover Design
& Book Layout
by Tom Rhule
Charleston, WV

We gratefully acknowledge the assistance of West Virginia Career College at Morgantown for providing facilities needed during the original preparation of this work.

Printed in the USA on recycled paper, by the Employee Owners of Thomson-Shore in Dexter, Michigan.

INTRODUCTION

Vietnam. Yesterday or ancient history? Americans of military age during this last war fought largely by draftees will never forget the impact it had -and still has- on their lives. Citizens born after the end of military conscription need give little thought to the realities of war beyond attending an occasional parade, standing proudly as jets fly over before athletic events, and voting for politicians who promise to "support the troops".

This state of affairs is not acceptable in a nation even nominally committed to lofty principles of freedom and democracy. Only the most naive and idealistic would argue that we should do away with our armed forces. It is equally naive and idealistic to expect those in power, those who vote or hold political office, to understand the nature of war if they have never served in the military or faced the reality of being compelled to do so. Praises aplenty can be heaped upon our now all volunteer military, but it is an undeniable reality that an all volunteer force has lifted the burden of knowledge and experience of the rigors of war from our citizenry. Those who send our forces into battle to shed the blood of war have increasingly little understanding of what they do. Literally, they have no skin in the game.

Veterans who served in the Vietnam era military were drawn from a broad cross section of our citizenry. Many were conscripted and no few of those who enlisted did so in the hope of avoiding ground combat. Others volunteered out of genuine patriotic zeal. Vietnam vets hoped to come home and resume their lives. Sadly, tens

i

of thousands did not return home alive and those who did were forever changed. A signature characteristic of those who returned has been silence. Nearly four decades after the end of the war, surviving Vietnam veterans remain silent to all but their closest confidantes -mainly fellow vets. This understandable silence has come at a terrible price. Citizens of the nation with the world's most powerful military no longer understand the nature of war. We can now enter into armed conflict with little real understanding among the citizenry of what is being done in our name and with our consent both to those of distant lands and to our neighbors.

This small volume, first compiled in 1977, offers a rare glimpse into the personal nature of armed conflict. Contributors to this work held and likely still hold wildly divergent political views. No matter. What we offer here is a candid look at war as seen by the participants. No grand ideologies or geopolitical analysis -plenty of such to be found elsewhere. Readers are not promised a "good read". Many over the years have been unable to finish this work -Too intense! It's rough! Indeed. It is supposed to be. Deal with it. Maybe it will save a few lives down the road.

PREFACE TO FIRST EDITION

Early in 1977 about 40 of us found ourselves thrown together several hours a week with rather loose instructions to "learn speech" -whatever that meant. We were virtually all coerced/enticed to do a speech course. The vast majority expecting to clear a tidy sum from V.A. educational benefits; a few were promised job advancement for furthering their education; I got paid to teach the course. It didn't take long to run the gamut from "this is what I did over vacation" to "now I will arose your emotions". Even less time was required for all concerned to tune out the various speakers.

Believing that learning could also be enjoyable, the focus daily shifted from "give a speech" to "communicate, tell a story". Invariably the stories came. We each had many to tell -few speeches but lots of stories. Our stories always centered around the same topic, the war in Southeast Asia. We were all members of that group of citizens most directly affected by the war: military lifers, draft age men, and enlisted personnel at the time of the war. As Appalachians, we represent a region traditionally called upon to supply a disproportionate number of military personnel during times of conflict. Yet seldom, if ever, have Appalachians who served in the military taken time to reflect, to tell their story. Soon the tape recorder was unboxed and we had each kicked in two dollars to cover the cost of tapes and a typist to transcribe them. Our story, an oral history, was becoming.

We each vouch for the authenticity of the tales you are about to read. They reflect, to the best of our recollection, events that actually occurred to us. Our names are not affixed to our individual stories for reasons which we believe the reader will understand. No attempt was made to form a group consensus on the war. Some of us are proud. Some are not. Some would do it again. Some would not. Some are willing to send their children. Some are not.

We did not start the war. We did not legislate the war. We did not command the war. Rather, each in our own role, be it chosen or forced, we fought the war. In the most real sense, it was our war. This is our story. We believe it needs to be told. We share it in the hope that Appalachians will never again go 'Cross the Pond.

EDITORIAL NOTE

The original transcriptionist was directed to type exactly from the tapes. These stories are printed as originally transcribed. Stories may begin or end with small amounts of extraneous material generated in the taping process or blanks where tapes were not audible. Fonts and spacing have been adjusted from the original admittedly crude work but substantive edits have been avoided. The editorial process, once begun, often takes on a life of its own. We chose not to take the risk. Changes for "clarity" can erode authenticity. This is a primary source oral history that happens to be in print. The goal is for the reader to "hear" these words as spoken.

THE AUTHORS

Don Auvil	Industrial worker
Kathy Barnette	Cashier
Glen Bee	Chemical worker
Roy Brewer	Truck driver
Don Bucklew	Coal miner
Steve Campbell	Pipe fitter
John Cox	Coal miner
Ralph Curfman	Coal miner, USAF ret.
Joe Donham	Food store manager
Charles A. Dow, Jr.	Coal miner
John Eisentrout	Coal miner
Ed Friel	Glass worker, shipping
Larry Greathouse	Construction worker
Regis Hardin	
Joe Hardy	Coal miner
John Hardy	Power station operator
Larry Harper	
Robert Hickman	
Gene Hill	Concept design
Eli Jabour	Postal worker
Roger Johnson	
Terry Johnson	Coal miner
Ron Kyle	Fireman
William Lemley	Coal miner
Lewis McConnaughey	Federal meat inspector
George McCormick	Heating & plumbing foreman
Rose McGrath	Medical photographer
Rick McMasters	Coal miner
Al Matteo	Farmer, US Army, ret.
Virgil Maxwell	Truck driver
Bill Menear	Power station operator

Roger Miker	Coal miner
Dave Mitter	Coal miner
John Morgan	Insurance sales manager
Susan Raygoza	Student
Larry Rose	Fireman
Andy Shartzer	Unemployed
Harvey Shrout	Coal miner
Steve Smith	Welder
Harry Snyder	Federal corrections officer
Earl Stewart	Restaurant owner
Dave Toothman	Coal miner
Ron Watson	Power station worker
Robert Welch	Fireman

THE FIRST FIRE FIGHT

The first fire fight I was ever in over there, we was coming up on this village and we was coming across the rice paddies. The village was built up in like a wooded area and they started firing at us out of the village so it was the first time I had ever been in one, you know, and we got up into the village and you couldn't see who was firing at you. You couldn't see nobody, but they was firing because there was a couple of tanks sitting out in a line, you know. So we just kept firing right into the wooded area and the buildings and that and all of a sudden, this pig come out and started running across in front of the tanks and everybody just forgot about the enemy and everybody started firing at that pig. That pig was running down across the line and we kept missing. I started firing at it too.

BY MYSELF PULLIN' COMBAT

I'm number nine and I want to talk about the training or lack of that I had when I went to Vietnam. I was trained to be a mechanic on engineering equipment so I got there – I got to Vietnam. I was there for two weeks in orientation, getting adjusted to the country and getting my orders and things. Went up north to my camp, which was Camp Red Devil. My first night there – I was there – I checked in – about an hour later they called me for guard duty. Two guys took me out and they showed me, you know, where my post was and they gave me a Claymore, which I had never seen before. He told me to go set it up, so it's dark and I found out later that the Claymore does have something written on it that tells you the directions on it. But anyway, they gave me the Claymore and they was going to go back and watch the movie and then the second show, I was going to go back and watch it. So here I am by myself pullin' combat. I thought I was a trooper, so I'm sittin' out there and went out and set the Claymore up and ran the wire back and had it detonated and so I was there about an hour and a half and finally, they came back. So we were talkin' before I was going to go back and he asked me what I was doing with all this equipment on and I said, "Well, aren't you supposed to wear this on guard duty?" And he says, "No." He had a tee-shirt on, I believe, and he was carrying a case with him. I had no idea what he had in the case. I'd never seen a weapon look like this. Finally, he opens the case up and pulls his trumpet out and he's sittin' there playin' his trumpet and I said, Well, I'm goin' to go back and watch the second movie." He said, "Did you set the Claymore up?" And I said, "Yeah." He told his buddy, "We better go check it." So here we went out and I had it set up. If I would have detonated it, it would have wiped me out because I had it turned right toward me, and this is a prime example of some people, you know, they went over there, trained for one job and they stuck them in another job.

DOWN IN ME THO, BACK IN '65

Down in Me Tho, back in '65, we pulled in there one night and couldn't get back to our camp. Stayed all night in Me Tho and while we were there they picked up a young VC. The brought him in. The ARVN's came and in the meantime – they was trying to get information out of him and I heard screaming in a little building off next to the runway that they had this man in. When I went in, well, I turned around and came out. I couldn't stand it. They had a regular fuel pump. They had one of those wires wrapped around his privates and another one they had stuck in his back and they were cranking that thing, trying to get that man to talk and that poor old man did some jumping you wouldn't believe. He was trying to get away from that fuel pump. He moved too far they just hit him with a rifle and knocked him back down and they operated on that man like that pretty close to two hours, two or three hours and an American captain that was there as an advisor gave them the order to go ahead and shoot that man and get him out of his misery and they wouldn't do it. So he shot the man.

THE RAT CAGE

I spent a good bit of time in Vietnam, something like four years total. '65 to '71 and in early, well '65, I remember a case I call the rat cage. We got a call from a village chief that they was paradin' a man through the village down there – an American – through a village below Me Tho and this man was stripped naked and was – he had a string tied around his privates and they was jerkin' this man through the streets. He was seen in Me Tho. He was seen a little farther down in a little place called Ki Bay and every time, naturally, we got a report, we would put up two or three gun ships and go try to find this man. We knew he was American. He was a big man. He was sandy-haired and one day we found him and they did have a man. He was an American lieutenant. He was being drug through the streets by the local Vietcong. We got him outside of Ki Bay and he had a bird cage built around his head and in that bird cage was three rats and he had his ears eaten off and part of his nose eaten off where those rats had been eatin' on this man when we went and got him.

Another case about a month after that, the Seventh Division – ARVN Division – we had a young man in. He was a SFC. He come in and went down to this division as an advisor. One day they went on operations and were going down to U Men Force and on the way down there, they got in some heavy contact and he was on a radio on the ground giving directions. We was takin' fire in covering the operations on the tree line and all at once Parker hollered over the radio, "I don't see nobody, there ain't a damn person here but me." And a few minutes later he called back and said, "I'm by myself. I don't know where I'm at. Get a gun ship down here and pick me up. There's not a soul with me." Then he said, "No, don't land. Here they come. There's ten of them coming after me. They are V.C.. They've got me by the arms." The radio went off. We didn't see any more of him until about three years later we found him tied to a tree where he had just starved.

DRINKING WATER

Talking about eightballs. SP-6 Smith was a real good man. I bailed him out of Three Quarter Cav. They busted him for pushing dope, brought him over to my outfit, gave him a job as a tech inspector on aircraft for all them planes and we moved out of our base camp on operations one night and we ended up in Long Binh and I gave him a job on this operation of driving a water tank. I couldn't see how he could possibly get in trouble driving a water truck. So I gave him a water truck and he's doing a pretty good job at it two or three days and one night late I went to the club and as I came back by the water truck this water truck coughed real loud and I got a little worried. I stopped and looked that water truck over pretty good and it coughed again. So I immediately jumped up, pulled the top of the tank open and found three women in there and this son of a gun had those women out in the field and was making a bundle off of those women. He kept them in our water truck. We were drinking water out of that.

THE FIRST TIME

Okay. This is me again. The guy stationed in Thailand. And when I first got to Thailand, a couple of my buddies met me there. The first day we went to the Airman's Club and we were drinking and we decided to go downtown. They decided to show me the town. So we went downtown and as soon as we got outside the gate, we noticed a massage parlor there. So I thought, well, you know, this is not for me. So we went on downtown and drank some and about a week or two later, I said, "Oh well, what the hell, I'll go to the massage parlor and give it a try." So we walked in. Me and my room mate walked into this massage parlor and we walk in and this guy was in there behind this wee little bar and he wanted to know if you want a drink. And on the left side we saw nothing but glass – see through glass stuff, you know, one sided mirrors like and all these bunch of girls in there. There must have been twenty or twenty-five of them. An they're all sitting in there in these little short skirt outfits and short outfits combing their hair and watching television and stuff and they don't see you and they all got a big number on them. It's like, you know, walking into a big Egyptian or Arabian night-sheik or something, you know. It was really funny and what you did, you told the guy, "Hey, I'll take number such and such." And he gets on this microphone and calls her out and she takes you to this room and the first time, you know, you don't know what to do. You're just kind of standing there in this room and it's got like a bed in it, a regular old massage table and you're standing there and you don't know what's going on. You don't know whether to take your clothes off or run like hell or what. So the first time I went, I said, "Well, I'll just take my clothes off." So I took my clothes off and hung them behind the door and she come in, she got a bath started and she gives you a bath and you know, you're feeling all funny, some strange chick doing all this stuff to you. Then she gets you on the table and gives you a massage and after that it's up to you whatever you want, you know, and you used to pay about five bucks for two hours. That included all services and it was a pretty unique experience the first time. It got old after a while though. That's about it.

SUPPLIES

I want to talk a little bit about supplies. After I was over there about five months my boots finally gave up and died so I needed a new pair of boots and I didn't have anything but a set of low quarters, so I went to the supply sergeant and he couldn't fix me up right then. He said I'd have to hold on. So I said, "okay, I'd go ahead and wear my low quarters" and I did for a while but that didn't last very long because I got myself a good set of blisters, block blisters. Some of you all probably had them, too. So I had to go over to the doctor, to a field hospital and they confirmed that I did have myself a nice set of blisters and everything. Said I ought to get me some better shoes. I said, "Well, that would be all right but I can't get hold of any, if you could help me out in some way." He said, "Yeah, I can give you some advice" and I thought he was going to help me out, maybe send a letter through or something, you know. But he told me to go down to the black market and I went to the black market the next time I was in town and I bought a set of boots as it so happened that was the only set of boots that I got while I was there the rest of the time. And I never got a set of boots until I got back to the United States.

GROUND POUNDERS

The first time I was over there I was on a helicopter and we used to take a lot of the dignitaries around – the high brass of the 101st around their unit. The 101st was continually getting their ass whipped. They was up in the Thieu _____ Valley. Just boys was all they were and this C Company, First of the 327th, got the hell beat out of them bad. So after it was all over they had the dignitaries come up there – like high brass and so forth. They wanted to know how in the hell this happened, you know, to one of their better fighting units. We were told by being in this helicopter outfit, you guys have the conveniences, the laundry was close by, you keep clean uniforms on all the time. You keep your boots shined up all the time. So here you go out, you got pressed fatigues on, you got shined shoes on and you smell like a rose and you go out and here's these God-damned grubby guys. They been out there for three months and never even taken a bath. The only water they got they kept to drink because there wasn't a stream or anything close by them and they smelled, they stunk, they looked grubby. Guys having big scratches on the side of their faces because you could tell they had to dry shave before these brass come out and these brass were the same way I was. All clean shaven and smelling like a rose and clean clothes on and they were out and they decided to dig in some of this shit, about how did this happen. How was you so stupid to let something like this happen? Still yet I knew damn well they gained their rank prior to Vietnam happening over there. So they go over there, a full bird or lieutenant general or something like that and they want to go out.

11

They want to know why these men let something like this happen.

The Vietcong for three nights prior to that night ran water buffalo through their security. There was this big herd of water buffalo there in the valley running wild. They weren't wild animals, but they were just – nobody claiming them and they herded those damn animals together and run them through their outside perimeter. Well, the first night, you know, they took a couple of shots. Everybody was jumpy but they seen those water buffalo so they calmed down. The next night the same thing. The third night everybody was joking about it. Hey, it's about time for the water buffalo to come through and here they came. On the fourth night, there was Vietcong with satchel charges, A-K and so forth and they were mixed in with the water buffalo. Here come those water buffalo and nobody even paid attention to them. Well, they went clear inside to where their communication bunker was even before somebody noticed that these dinks were running around in among those water buffalo and there was three platoons of men out there, one hundred twenty men, and I think they had something like sixty dead, something like thirty or forty wounded. There was just a very few men walking around unscratched and I've never particularly – this one person, a colored guy, he looked like a mountain and he was about six two or three, about two thirty to two forty pounds. I was wondering what the hell he was doing on the ground pounders, being so damned big. He looked like a football player and I remember, it wasn't a couple of months before that he went out on a chopper that I was gunning on, re-supplies to them, bringing, you know, new men and so forth and supplying them and this guy was on that chopper because I remember him. He was so damn big and when the Vietcong come through and done all their damage, on their way out, every soldier that they got, they shot right in the forehead and that was just psychological, you know. You'd see, you'd say, "Oh my God, look what these guys done." They shot every one of them in the head, you know. They must really be some crack shots and all this, just to make your mind – anyway, it was our chopper that went out about two weeks later to pick up the dead and he was one of them and I remember, he had that God-damned big hole in the middle of his forehead and you know, you talk about brass coming out and how did they understand what goes on out in the field? That was it right there. They had no idea what actually going out there and staying two or three months at a time without a bath and so forth, but still yet they could take the time to come out and chew somebody's ass out for not doing their job right. That's it.

TIME IN A MILITARY HOSPITAL

I did a little bit of time in a military hospital in Pensacola, Florida when I got back to the states. There was seventy of us in this one ward. Most of the guys had a leg amputated or an arm chopped up pretty bad. I was lucky. I just had a hand and arm injury and I was the only one in that whole ward that could walk on my own without a cane or a crutch or a wheelchair but the spirits were up pretty good in that hospital. We didn't have much to do after morning. I walked around and picked up all the trash and did what I could since I could use my feet and after we got the place cleaned up, which we did ourselves – we had one nurse that was in charge of the seventy guys in the hospital and she kept pretty busy running around giving everyone their medication and stuff. So we took pretty good care of ourselves. But we had this one old guy named Jake and he was shot up pretty bad in the lower crotch area and they had him in a body cast and his legs spread apart and a bar between his legs to hold them that way and he was pretty well immobile but he was a happy-go-lucky guy. We always helped him in the morning and that would make his legs stick straight up in the air and we got us a piece of plywood about three feet square and we just put it right on top of his cast and we'd all gather around and play cards. That was funny, trying to see a guy – we just played hearts and spades, something that you had to hold about fourteen or fifteen cards and you could only use one hand. After you was in there a couple of months you'd be surprised how good you could get with one hand. You could hold a whole hand of cards and throw the card you wanted without dropping them.

Poor old Jake. He couldn't fit out the doors because his legs were spread. He was in that body cast and after about noon, we always went up on the top floor of the hospital where we could get some sunshine. So I'd wheel Jake and we had a marine in front of us on a cane and he'd hobble along and kick open the double doors and then I could only wheel him with one arm and I would kick my foot under the wheelchair and get him up on one wheel and he would kind of balance himself and we would send him out those double doors sideways, so he could fit. It was pretty funny, when it all happened. Well, Jake got to leave after I was there about two months and we did it the same way. His dad and mom came to get him to put him in a station wagon. I don't know how far he had to ride. I didn't know him personally before I was over in 'Nam, but his dad and mom really got a kick out of seeing us put him in that station wagon for him to ride home when we kicked him up on the side like that. But most guys over there, even when they are shot up bad and when they get back to the States, it's hard to believe how good of spirits they really do have even with no legs or one leg. It's hard to believe how well you accept what's happened to you.

We even had one guy that was in had both legs amputated, got married. He was in a bed next to me and he didn't know me from Adam until I got there but he asked me to be his best man and I was and him and his wife spent a glorious week and a half in the isolation ward by theirselves and the Navy didn't say nothing to them. They offered it to them and they gladly accepted it. It was funny, I tell you.

PAPERWORK

I was in the United States Navy from 1966 to 1970. I spent one year at WESTPAC, one year in the Med. and two years in the States. I want to talk a little bit about paperwork and waste. Over in WESTPAC we had a nonrep about every two weeks because we used a _____ ordinance, planes. One particular time I was a second class pay officer in charge of the forward magazines and took inventory on these once a week. This particular time I reported to our gunner that we had 750 five inch Zuni rocket motors that cost about one thousand dollars a piece. He said, "We only have paperwork for 500 Zuni rocket motors." I told him, "Well, we have 750." He turned and looked at me with a straight face and he said, "We have 500 Zuni rocket motors tomorrow." Tomorrow, the next day, we had 500 five inch Zuni rocket motors and under the ship, the night before, we had 250 – approximately two hundred fifty thousand dollars of taxpayer's money wasted.

I COULDN'T TURN IT IN

In Saigon, a few years back, we had a couple of warrant officers in the city. They had overnight passes. They stayed overnight and they stayed an extra day. So the next evening they decided they better come back. They went down to the air field and no helicopters were there to bring them back so they just politely got in an aircraft and flew it out. They were my pilots. They stole an aircraft, they pulled in a hangar, left it there and then decided they couldn't get rid of it. They didn't know what to do with it so they talked me into changing the tail numbers on it and I used that aircraft for about seven months as a maintenance float –maintenance aircraft and personal aircraft.

The division that this aircraft belonged to closed down and left Vietnam, but one aircraft short. Immediately after that, my unit closed down and I was transferred to another unit north of where I was at, next to Saigon. I took this aircraft with me and I used that aircraft the remainder of my time there, some four months, and we closed down and I had a problem. I'm sittin' here with a $2000 helicopter. I couldn't turn it in, nobody would take it. It was an illegal aircraft; every component on it was over time change. So this 79th Maintenance unit we turned it in to, decided they would have a _____. Anything you had, you could turn it in, no questions asked. We flew that thing down there and landed and the colonel of that place went absolutely crazy. He didn't want that aircraft. Didn't want anything to do with it, but he's the one that made the deal and we politely walked away.

PURPLE HEARTS

This is a story about purple hearts. I knew two people in 'Nam who got purple hearts. One guy fell off a building and broke his leg running for cover. The other guy got shrapnel in his leg. The guy that got shrapnel in his leg didn't get anything because he was bombed by American bombers. The guy who fell off the roof and broke his leg got a purple heart because he was running for the bunkers – they were being attacked and he didn't have any choice. He just ran right off the edge.

NO CUSTOMS

I want to say something about misappropriation of government funds and this was close, pretty close, to the close of the war. I was stationed at Clark Air Force Base. Our outfit was picked to be in charge of all the Far East for refueling purposes. On our return everybody had to go through customs and our outfit was exempt from customs because the Secretary of the Air Force, or Secretary of Defense got (indistinguishable) an airplane load of furniture for him so we went and picked up the furniture and was twenty aircraft in our outfit was coming back. We flew into Guam. Well, I was in charge of all the personnel on those twenty aircraft. One aircraft didn't have no personnel on it which we could carry around forty-five people because of the furniture that belonged to the Secretary of Defense.

Well, we wanted to make a whiskey run and Guam was the last place for cheap whiskey before you hit the States. Well, they said since the state you're stationed in only allows you to bring a fifth back, this is all you can bring back. I said, the United States said each man can bring a gallon in. The aircraft commander said nobody was going to bring in no whiskey and put it on the aircraft. I said, I'm in charge of the people and we'll see about this. So I got hold of my wing commander and I was taking care of the Secretary of Defense's furniture so I said I got about five hundred people down here that's waiting at the liquor store to buy whiskey, and all of those aircraft commanders are not going to let them buy whiskey, but yet they went and bought whiskey. I think they was bringing back four or five gallons and wanted people that didn't drink to sign their declaration form. I said nobody's signing anything. So he said let me talk to the aircraft commander. He said, I'll tell him what to tell the rest of them. So he told him, he said, each man will have a gallon of whiskey and he said it will not revoke customs. There is no aircraft in this fleet is going to go through customs. Landed in the States. No customs. The customs officials was there and signed each release for each aircraft but we was exempt from customs all the way through, each place signed our release but we got our whiskey and the Secretary of Defense got his furniture.

TWO BIG SUMP HOLES

Operation Hobo. We was on Hobo Wood. We took a gaggle of aircraft in there. A whole bunch of soldiers. The whole First Cav – the 25th Infantry Division went in and we had a lot of action in that place. We was pinned down for something like two days and I was flying helicopter recovery and running out of base camp. Well, in the meantime, they brought these great big containers in. They was using them for field hospitals and they was bringing these men back out of the field pretty regular, a lot of them, and the doctors, well, they called it first aid, was absolutely amputating. If a man come in with an arm that was shot and I didn't even consider it seriously, they would cut that arm off and they closed that operation down. We had two big sump holes that were something about ten by twelve foot deep full of limbs and things and we would burn them. But I thought it was unnecessary and I believe that it was just absolutely no reason to do all that amputating that they did.

WE DIDN'T DO ANY OF THAT STUFF

We didn't have any medics on our boat. When we went out to sea, fairly close to the land of 'Nam, I rode, oh, the same thing as a riverboat only it was just a patrol boat for the ship. We patrolled the area one mile in diameter of the carrier and we had a bullhorn and you always hear these stories, fire shots across the bow and stuff like that. Well, we didn't do any of that stuff. We didn't use the bullhorns. I was Aviation. _____ was my second class and I was a machine gunner on that boat. I don't ever remember of shooting any VC because we hardly ever seen any. But there's been countless number of junks, women and children, and they just give the order to fire and that's what we did do.

THE DENTIST

I was, well, in '67 and '68 I was stationed in about four or five different places. When I was in Saigon during the Tet Offensive we had a clerk. He was a pretty nice guy but as soon as everything started to get heavy, he just snapped and they had called him the dentist. We had a big fight right in the streets of Saigon and after it was over, there was a body count of abut three hundred fifty. There were North Vietnamese, Vietcong, and he always went along with – well, he had a little bag that he used to take out gold teeth, put them inside the bag. He'd go along to the bodies and open their mouths. If they had any gold teeth, he'd pull them and a couple of guys they found this one VC, the head was off and they tucked it's head back to where it was supposed to be and put the shirt around it. And he came along, too, and stepped on his chest and opened up his mouth and put the pliers on it and it come straight up like this and that kind of cooled him down for a while. He went back to the hospital. But they let him out. After we got back to the base, he grabbed a fifty caliber machine gun and went up on top of the hill with it and started firing down at our compound and the only way they could get rid of the situation was shoot back at him. So they opened fire on him and killed him.

THEY LET HIM GO

I was assigned to the 245th Surveillance Plane Company in Da Nang. It was an army reconnaissance unit. They flew army Mohawks and so on and we had a helicopter unit right next to us and they were all fighter helicopters. I guess one of the worst experiences I ran into in Da Nang. We had the compound full of Vietnamese people all day long until five or six o'clock in the evening. They were on clean up detail all the time. I packed parachutes on the flight line for the ejector seat in the army Mohawk. Well, the Vietnamese weren't supposed to be out on the flight line at all. They were just supposed to be within the living quarters and I caught a young man out on the flight line drawing a map – a complete layout of the flight line, you know, and after he'd get his bearings on the flight line, he's turn around and back away from the compound towards the mountains. He'd pick out a landmark and mark it on the map too. So I took him to the Battalion Commander at the Battalion Headquarters. I turned him over to a GE-2. They let him go. They let him leave the compound that night with the rest of the Vietnamese. Three o'clock in the morning, we was under rocket attack and I've got pictures to show how well they can hit their targets from the map. I got pictures of army Mohawks with tail sections blowed clear off of them. Helicopters that were completely destroyed on the flight line. The only use we had for the hangar was for repairs. We didn't park the planes in the hangars and the helicopters, naturally, we kept all them and they were only surrounded by 55 gallon drums full of sand. There was no top over them at all and all because they let this gook go.

GOING TO NORTH VIETNAM

We were going to North Vietnam en route to a mission that after so many battles of just pushing the enemy back and then back off and wait, push the enemy back when they come up again. The same old story. Lose men but pay for the same territory for the second time with more lives. We did this five times before we had a C.O. who was in the Korean War had been through every ounce of training that you could possibly get in the military service, and he said, "I will not pay for any more land with lives." He says, "I will not go through that again." He says, "As General Patton said, I won't pay for the same territory twice. I'll only pay it once." He asked for forty-two volunteers and got them. Our job was to go out and search out and destroy anything and everything that got in our path and he wanted to cut a twenty-five mile wide path from our position, fifty miles north and annihilate anything in between. We did that. With no connection with Lieutenant Calley, who in all of our opinions was unjustly tried and unjustly imprisoned and is still in a mess that he should never have been in. General Westmoreland did issue orders to search and destroy and I feel that Calley is innocent of any charges brought against him and his statement that he was following orders is exactly true. After this mission, we received eighteen more missions to do the same thing. Search and destroy. Annihilate anything and everything that moves, whether it be man, woman, child, animal, village, military strategic command or anything. Well, if it moves, destroy it. If it doesn't move and looks like it would harbor arms, equipment or anything, level it.

FUNERAL DETAIL

All right, I don't know how many people here ever been on a funeral detail, but when I was stationed at Laredo, Texas, they called up and said they needed so many men for a funeral detail and being in the Air Force, most of the clothes I had were just wash and wear – just washed them and wore them – never worried about ironin' them. So they come out and said you had to have everything pressed in "15 till 5" uniforms, they called them that we wore up there. And we took a bus up to Lampasos, Texas, and we took beer up with us, stopped off at some place and bought some beer – was drinking and having a good time so we had about six or seven hours before we was supposed to go to the funeral home, pick the body up, go ahead and take it to the cemetery and we really never thought anything about it.

We thought everything was going to be just a complete duty, go back, you know, no change. We get to the funeral home, you know, all funerals aren't the prettiest thing in the world. If you have ever been to a military funeral, it's got one hell of a moving feeling over a person. Our lieutenant that went up with us, he was the only one that could play the taps on the bugle and his name was Chad Everett. So my duty was as the men brought the casket in, the draped casket, out of the hearse and brought it over, what you call it, the rafters or whatever it is that hold the casket over top the hold, and as they played the taps, they went ahead and folded back the flag. My job was that I was to take the flag, make the last fold in it, do an about face and present it to the mother or father.

Well, like I said, if you have ever been there, when they play the taps, I think everybody there including yourself, got tears in their eyes. I mean everybody crying and it just seems like it's got to be the strangest feeling anybody can go through. So after I made the last fold and made an about face, the woman wouldn't take the flag. She was crying and she was – I was afraid she was going to hit me there for a while. I didn't know whether she was going to grab me, I didn't know how to react under the circumstances, because I was at attention presenting the flag to her. I guess her sister, or whatever came up and bailed me out. She came up and took the flag off of me and after we went ahead and we stepped back away from the coffin and after the taps are played, everybody does an about face and marches out and then they go ahead, the people pay their last respects by placing a rose or whatever on top of the casket. I think there must have been two cases of beer – that was about an eight hour drive back to Laredo, Texas, and when we got to the base I think we still had about two cases of beer. I don't think there wasn't too many conversations on the drive back down there. We never knew the guy, but after going through something like that, the emotional feeling was 100% reversible. What a change.

KNIFE HAPPY

In January, 1968, to November, 1968, I was assigned to _____. Okay, again in this _____ outfit that I was in, once in a while, whenever new troops would come in, I was platoon sergeant then and every so often when new men would come in I'd have to take them out on training missions just to get them familiar with the jungle and so forth – the area around our fire base and this person, in particular, I remember real well. His name was Florez and he was Mexican-American and Florez was one of those guys that was given a choice of spending two years in the Army or going to prison. He was arrested for knifin' a guy in California somewhere. Anyway, Florez, he always spoke broken English and was always kind of funny listenin' to him talkin' and while we was out on this training mission, he always wanted to talk on the radio. Nobody could understand the damn guy.

So after three or four training missions, the captain asked me if these particular people were ready to go out on a mission and I'd tell him yeah, most of the time. Sometimes I'd tell him no, they needed some more. So this one time they were short on team leaders – a couple of them had got shot up a little bit and they was just in the field hospital there. So he told me I had to take a team out. Well, I'd done this before so I didn't mind it and he told me to take Florez with me. So we were – it was just a recon mission – five men – all we was supposed to do was watch this area. It was a Montigard village and they wanted to know, toward evening especially, if we seen anybody walkin' in and out of that place with weapons. So we was out there about three days and saw nothing. Just people coming in and out – just looked like an ordinary village.

I was about ready to give up and call in and tell them we thought it was useless and just right before dark one evening, here come this Montigard walkin' down the trail and he had an ammo belt around his waist and he had some home made grenades on him in a pack. So when he got down to where we were all concealed, we stood up and he stopped and we had a Montigard interpreter with us and this interpreter kept asking him what he did with his weapon – what he done with his rifle – it was carbine ammo that he had and we was always kind of anxious to try to get hold of any kind of weapons just to keep them. So the only thing this Montigard done, he just kept smilin'. He had a big rotten teethed smile and I was standin' there and I was gettin' kind of mad about the whole thing because we weren't supposed to take prisoners.

The only thing we was supposed to do was watch and we'd done gave that up when we all stood up and Florez, he was always a little knife happy. He'd get in an argument back around the fire base if he was drunk and he'd pull a knife on you and he was proud of this big damn Bowie knife he had about that long. I was standin' there and I said, for just no reason at all – I didn't really mean it, I said, "Somebody ought to wipe the smile off that bastard's face." Just as soon as I said that, here was a gurgling sound – it just sounded like somebody was gargling – and I turned around and there that man's head was layin' back on his pack and just about three or four

29

inches of the meat was still holding his head on and Florez was standin' there with a big damn smile on his face. I said, "Florez, what the hell did you do that for?" And he said, in this broken English, "You said wipe the smile off his face." He said, "That's all I done" and that was it.

HARDEST LOOKING HOG

I was there in '66,'67. I was with an armored outfit. I was a tank driver. We'd be sent to – our platoon had been sent down or near Saigon to guard an ammunition dump that had been hit. There was only four of us guarding those facilities and they had us spread out pretty thin around the perimeter of the thing and it's set up where one night you did four hours. Two of us would have four hours of guard and the other two would have eight hours of guard for the night. Well, my tank commander run into some friends that were stationed near there and every night they'd come and get him and he'd go down and party and every other night I had four or eight hours of guard to pull.

We was there two or three weeks. I'm not sure now. I can't remember. But they pulled us in and gave us what amounted to the night off and he was headed for downtown and I told him I was going with him and he started hassling me about it but I said as much guard as I pulled for you, I said, I'm going with you. So we hit the village. I'd never done it before but I actually drank myself sober. I can remember going into the club. It's the South Vietnamese Army Officer's Club, but any G.I. can get in and I remember sitting there drinking, oh, man, just as hard as I could drink and I lost it about ten o'clock and about twelve, twelve thirty or something like that it was just like I came to and somebody pattin' my hand.

It had to be the hardest looking hog I ever saw while I was over there setting there pattin' my hand and in the meantime, we still didn't give up. We sat there and drank and it must have been three o'clock in the morning before we finally decided to leave. No weapons. We were out where we shouldn't been and no transportation to get us back to where we was supposed to be. So the two of us started up this village street there. Just like we was monkeys, running because it was the only way we were going to get back in time was to run and any time we saw a vehicle coming, naturally, we had to hide because we didn't know if it was the M.P.s or who the devil it was and we came across a hootch that was all lit up. I was just about half here and half gone, you know. I couldn't figure out what was going on. The sergeant, he knew and he stopped. I didn't have much choice but to stop with him and he finally told me it was a wake and like I said, up until that point I had no idea what it was and he told me that and I got to looking around for the body and I saw an old woman laying on a couch here. If she wasn't dead she was missing the best chance she ever had because I'm sure that had to be the corpse laying there and all this stuff going on around me going on and that's the only thing I could watch was that body sitting there and finally the old woman stirred and started to set up and just about scared me to death and I finally wander around there a little bit and found the casket.

We had an awful lot of fun trying to get back that night. We made it, but just barely. Several times we had to run off the road and the sergeant, he'd got into some rice whiskey there while we was at the wake and he was really out of it and every time something would come I'd have to knock him off of one side of the road and I'd run. We did that all the way back until the one particular time I seen lights coming and I shoved him off one side of the road and I went tearing in between two hooches but it was so damn dark I couldn't tell because they were on the ground there. There was a real steep bank and they were sitting up on stilts. It seemed like I fell one hundred feet before I finally hit the bottom and that's it, I made up my mind if they put me in jail, I ain't running off that road again.

COME TO FIND OUT...

I remember when they mined the harbor in Vietnam to stop the Russians from bringing in the supplies and stuff, you know, that they mined and I just thought, you know, at the time that the Navy had mined the God-damned harbor. Come to find out that B-52s came in and dropped these special – dropped these special bombs which were mines into the harbor and the mines were very sophisticated. They just didn't blow up like, you know, they show on TV or something where as a boat hits it the son of a bitch goes up but these, you know, you could go down and beat the hell out of the son of a bitch and it wouldn't go. It was, I guess, electronic or something they called it and it would count the ships and the big ships and the small ships, you know, the little boats, count them in and out of the harbor and after so many, whatever they had set the fuse for, after coming in and going out, so many times it would blow up and catch, you know, however many that it could coming out or coming in. That's about it.

SETTING UP AMBUSHES

Well, we were in Vietnam in '69 and came back in '70. I was in what they call a cav unit – marine units and what it consisted of, you had less than squads. Marines had about eight marines and what it boiled down to, you were supposed to give them on the job training to the PFs or pocket forces of South Vietnam. And what they consisted of was going out and setting up ambushes and stuff like that and running them through it. About three months later you'd get a new platoon. They'd switch them around so you could train them pretty well, but it seemed like every time we got a new platoon about the first three or four times you got hit they'd all run. What happened, you were sitting there with eight marines and maybe thirty PFs and they give you thirty-eight people and you spring your ambush on say twenty people and your PFs get up and run and that left eight marines against twenty Vietcong which didn't work out too well.

So what we used to do and did was every time we got a new platoon, for the first week or maybe two weeks, we always set up secure areas and about one or two o'clock in the morning, when they'd all be asleep when they was supposed to be up on the watch, we'd pull pins of grenades and just frag them until they got to the point where they didn't want to run any more and just about that time, you'd get them to the point where they didn't run or they'd act half way decent, they'd switch platoons around and you'd have to start all over again.

WHATEVER HAPPENED TO THEM

This is the same as before. You know, I went over in '69 and '70 and we had to train these PFs. Like I said, when you get hit all the time they always take off running and the next morning they'd show up. So we'd made a kill one night. I think it was three or four that we caught and we used to drag them up in the road and leave them there until morning and then, you know, whatever happened to them, somebody would come along and take them away and bury them or whatever.

The PFs used to come back in the morning after they took off and I remember this one particular incident, the guy was dead, you know, he'd been dead for a couple of hours and the PF used to get real brave after they was dead and one of the PFs came up and took the guy's leg – one of the guys that was dead – and laid it up on a rock and jumped on both his legs and broke his legs and then he cut off one of his fingers and took it with him. I don't know what he ever did with it but they used to get real brave after they – break their legs and stuff and I remember one night we killed a female VC and one of the PFs took one of those power techniques that, you know, get it in your hand and it shoots up in the air, a star cluster and shot it up her _____. You could just see her stomach gurgling and burning and shit like that when he did that.

TARGET FIXATION

I was aboard ship in '69 during our first line period. I believe it was when we were operated in the South China Sea. We had two squadrons that flew the same type of aircraft and many of the shops – the maintenance shops were consolidated – well, was consolidated with the other squadron in the shop that I worked in. And I guess one of the things that bothered me to some degree during that first line period, we were in night operations and our sister squadron had a young lieutenant junior grade as a branch officer, which I'd met him once or twice. I don't suppose he was more than maybe twenty or twenty-one years old. Really, he hadn't even begun to realize at all what life was even about and during one of the night operations apparently on a strafing run he got target fixation and flew into the ground. Of course, that was the end of him.

We lost a few other pilots while we were over there. I don't know that we lost any to actually being shot down in combat but nevertheless, whether they're shot down in combat or they crash into the sea as one of our better pilots did, they're still lost and there's no way to bring those fellows back. I thought what a waste, a young man twenty or twenty-one years old, having not even really begun to live yet and his life ended so abruptly simply because he was there doing his duty.

NEVER REALLY FINISHED

I spent eight and a half years in the navy and always, most of that time was in support of the war effort in Vietnam. However, in 1969, I spent most of the year aboard the aircraft carrier Kitty Hawk operated in the South China Sea. During the time we were there in 1969 the war was still going pretty heavy and we dropped, I don't know how many really, tons of, multiply thousands of tons of bombs, but we always were given the understanding that all the bombs we were dropping were not in Vietnam itself but in Laos and I suppose that over all the things that irritated me I guess about the war was the fact that during all those years of fighting in Vietnam, we never really finished the battle. Never really won the war and I suppose because politics played too big a role in it. I was never against, set against the idea of why we were there, what we were trying to accomplish, but I was and still am to this day a little irritated at the fact that we never finished the job we were to do. I realize there were a lot of injustices in the war and of course, in wars there always are but nevertheless I cannot see the justification in fighting a war where you have your hands tied behind you and yet the enemy on the other side are not tied in the same way.

I worked on the flight deck on the air carrier many days, loaded a lot of bombs. I didn't have to load bombs but I did it because I thought, well, this is my part toward just keeping the aircraft flying. I'd like to see these aircraft going off that deck loaded with bombs and come back empty. Not that I'm a sadist or anything of this nature but I felt like the war itself in many aspects was justified. I'd rather fight communists on their ground than in my own backyard. However, again, I still think that the war had too much politics in it. There was just too much graft. It really wasn't a war that was meant to be won by our country. In fact, I have often wondered what the purpose of it was other than maybe to boost the economy which is a sad note that expensive money lost lives.

NOBODY COULD EVER

In March of '68 I was stationed at Ma Me Thut and I drew an opinion while I was there that in some cases the enemy really had to be psyched up to do the things that it did. One night I was on this – on the berm – there was guard posts about every thirty or forty feet and we used to take turns. They had bunkers built right into the berm there and lights going out into the foliage and wire and we used to stay on top of the bunkers as we traded every hour or so guarding the compound and one night, I was sitting on top of the bunker and I seen the foliage move. About two o'clock position from where I was sitting and well, at first, I even, you know doubted that anybody would even attack, that we were so well fortified with weapons and so forth right at that particular part of the compound, that I thought surely nobody could ever do that, so I just kept watching.

I didn't really jump at any conclusions or anything because it was a little hard for me to believe anyway. So in a little while here comes two young Vietnamese jumping out – zappers – loaded with home made bombs and grenades and everything hung on them and they started charging that perimeter and I knew right then, I didn't even have to fire, because I knew what was going to happen and it just looked like – it looked like with the tracers. Every fifth round there was supposed to be a tracer. It looked like one big white hollow core going right into those two bodies as they approached that perimeter and naturally, there was nothing left of them but it really amazed me that – I, well, they just had to get wound up on something to do, something like that and when we got hit another night they were throwing mortars into a tube and throwing, you know, logging them in on us and they were going so fast I remember thinking to myself, they are pumping them too fast. There's going to be a mistake and surely enough, about two or three rounds later they had dropped one mortar in on top of another on the same tube when they were out and blew themselves complete to hell and back.

RAT PATROLS

I went to Vietnam in May 1968, and our headquarters was at Chu Lai. I was in the 198th Flight Infantry Brigade and I remember this one night we was pulling what they call rat patrols. We would go to one location, set up an ambush for three or four hours and then we'd move on maybe nine hundred meters away and set up another ambush. We did this all night long and in this area where we were at, they were firing rockets in on Chu Lai and we would set the ambush up and maybe catch them on the way carrying the rockets or whatever. But this one night, we were at the first location and the point man and sergeant up front they heard this activity and since our mission was ambushes, they decided that we would just go around this area and still get to our location.

So the sergeant decided to send back the word, back through the squad – well, there was two squads this night. There was sixteen or seventeen of us there. That the point that was going to come back, each man from the front would go to the rear and they started sending the word back to get back so far through the line and the word got turned around so the last three men they understood that they were to just turn around and go back. So they went back forty or fifty yards or something like this and it was a point man and sergeant that was coming back. I heard this sergeant yell, "Americans" and there was no answer and just a few seconds later, the point man, the sergeant and another man they each cut open on full automatic, twenty rounds a piece at the three men who had fell back and well, just lucky, that no one was killed. They were injured pretty bad.

A GOOD TIME

At the time I found out that I was getting drafted, I was dating a girl from the draft board and she said, "You're going in a couple of days" so I just went around to different branches of the service to find out where I could get the best deal. The Navy offered me the best deal. They offered me a school. I didn't have to sleep in any foxholes or eat any C-rations. I floated around the Caribbean for four years and just had one hell of a good time.

IN A BED

I was in the Vietnam war from 1967 to 1968 and I want to talk to you about the misappropriation of government bodies. When I was – I was shot in my last four months that I was in Vietnam and I went to Van Kou, in a hospital and during the time I was there, I've seen people come in missing arms, legs, different parts of their body and the worse thing that I saw there, there was a man that came in. He stepped on a land mine and he weighed seventy-two pounds at the time they brought him in. After they operated on him he lost twenty-two pounds and he was missing both of his arms, part of his face and from his waste down there was nothing. Just part of his intestines were hanging out. Just about every night you could hear him wanting to die. He begged and begged and begged but they just kept him alive.

It was found out later the only reason they kept him alive because they – different soldiers that came in, they were down on themselves and wanting to die because they were losing an arm or a leg or something, you know. They wanted them to look at him and see that they really wasn't that bad off because he was nothing there. You know, it was just terrible and another thing that I was mad about was different soldiers, you know, caught different diseases because of – I guess lack of control. They knew they wasn't supposed to go out and mess around with women carrying the disease but they got it anyway and the government, they would instead of trying to cure them, they knew they couldn't cure them because it was an incurable disease, they just wrote home through channels that their son was missing in action or he died in action, which he wasn't dead at all. They didn't want the disease to go back to the United States so they kept them over there and this was because I found – where I was working at, I seen the government papers where they actually said, your son is dead or your son is missing in action and he'd be lying in a bed beside of me.

NEVER KNOW

We had five individuals who were injured very badly over there. These individuals, as far as their families were concerned, are now and forever will be reported dead. The government is taking care of them along with some veterans from Korea and World War II and to my knowledge, World War I if they are still alive, but these people are people who have been physically or mentally deranged from an action, in an armed conflict and these people have all been reported dead and their families will never know that they are still living, but they are either mentally incapable of ever going home and it was their wish and desire to be reported dead to their families and never to be heard from again. When they are dead and buried they will be buried under their own names within another area, I think it is at least one thousand miles from where their homes are.

Wess: And you know of five of these from the one mission you were on in North Vietnam?

Yeah. There was five from our mission that were just placed in a home to be taken care of and they were reported dead to their families and any man who has gone through that has seen these people, would know, he would understand, and he'd keep the secret and their families will never be notified.

BASE CAMP

I'd like to tell about the same place he was talking about a little while ago, the Hobo Woods. We was on operation up there one day. We was operating out of Ku Che – the 25th Infantry Division. It was really to Ku Che and we was up at Hobo Woods and we got in a pretty big fight and when we was finished, we had one hundred fifteen body count and we was searching them and among this one hundred fifteen dead, there was about six North Vietnamese regulars, what I call hard core over there. The rest of them, the rest of the dead Vietcong or VC, every one of them had Ku Che identification cards, which means they probably worked on our base camp during the day, you know, and they were fighting us. They lived in the village of Ku Che and worked at our base camp and then they were out there fighting us. They all had i.d. cards to travel in our base camp.

THIS ONE GUY

I hadn't been there too long but they come out with the warning not to go downtown and spend the night with any of the women down there because some of the women were pretty dangerous and this one guy, I think his name was Gonzales, but I can't swear to that, he decided that he wasn't going to pay any attention to them. He was going to go downtown and he was going to – because before this, before the Tet Offensive and the May Offensive of '68, they'd go downtown and spend, oh maybe, you didn't have to have a pass. As long as you were there for work the next day, but after that time you had to have a pass to get out of the air base and you weren't allowed to stay out all night, but this one guy, like I said, he decided he was going to stay downtown anyway, so he got away with it for a long time, but eventually it caught up with him and they found him downtown with a knife in his back. Needless to say, he didn't stay downtown anymore.

STORIES

I wasn't in Vietnam. I spent all my time on the east coast of the United States – around Fort Knox, Fort Bragg, Fort Eustis, Fort Lee – but I did come in contact with a lot of guys that were just coming back from Vietnam. My whole company in Fort Knox were Vietnam veterans returning and I came across a lot of stories that – and a lot of pictures. I guess they weren't allowed to bring them back but some of them did. They put them in the bottom of their duffle bags or something and this one guy in particular, he told me that he was out on a helicopter. He was in an Air Cav. unit and he was out flying around one day and he caught this Vietcong and caught him like a ground hog away from their hole and they were just trying to run but he said, you know, it's nothing for helicopters to run them down and they shot two of them. Killed them.

He told me just about two weeks later he went back and these bodies were still laying there. So he just returned, set down, and he got off and went over and pulled their heads off. Their bodies were, I guess, decomposed enough so that he didn't have much trouble and he told me he took those heads with him back to the compound there and cleaned them up and then safety wired them on to the skid tips of his helicopter and you know, I guess you see this helicopter come flying around, he said they were scared to death of copters anyway and they'd always try to outrun them but they never could do it.

And there's another thing, he was telling me about these young boys, I guess in Saigon and bigger places they didn't have any parents or their parents maybe got killed or something and they was running around in large groups. They called them _____ boys. Each time you would be walking down the street and you were alone, these big groups of young boys would come up and just beat the hell out of you. Just jump you all at once and take your money and grab your hat. It ain't worth anything.

Another thing that was pretty common from what I understand, the killing of your sergeants mostly. Guys would get, they'd get killed. While they was sleeping, see, if the guy was a sergeant and messing around with you or something and causing problems well, you just do him in, you know, take a hand grenade while he was sleeping and get him. Pop it in his door and take off and there was the end of him. There was one guy in particular told me he used Claymore mines for this. He put them in the wall right along this guy's bunk where he slept and he used two Claymore mines and I guess, did him in real quick, you know.

There's a lot of things that happened that a lot of people don't believe, but I've seen pictures like I said. I wasn't there, but I've seen pictures which proved it. Bodies and bowels, arms, legs, all parts, just strung out all over.

FUNNIEST THING

The funniest thing I had happen to me when I was in Vietnam. Well, it didn't happen to me, but I was on guard duty in Long Kou and that's an in-country R&R station and helicopters would come in to gas up. It was on the other side of the airport there. These two helicopters came in. They tried to beat each other in to the gas pumps and they got their beaters caught together and it flew them all over that place and they had to end up paying for them.

FOR EXCITEMENT

Well, for excitement, we used to get down around Tan Sanh Hut Air Base. They had a place down there where they trained the Vietnamese paratroopers and they had a tower with a parachute _____ and for excitement we used to go down there and watch them jump down and turn them loose. The wind would be blowing and about fifteen of the guys had to run and catch them because one guy couldn't handle the chute. It was funny. Seeing these guys down there running all over the field trying to catch each other.

DIDN'T NEED ANY

The only memorable experience that happened in Vietnam was when I was stationed in the Fourth Division in an _____ outfit. We had short patrols in our area of responsibility. What we did do was two types -there was just a plain recon patrol. We went out and watched and gathered information and reported it back and another one was an ambush mission where we just went out and tangled with them. On this one particular occasion, a team, there was five of us, and we went out and reconned the area by helicopter so we could get an idea of what we was going into and we went out and early one morning and was put in the helicopter, the landing zone. From there, there was about five hundred meters to the area that was picked out on the map for our ambush. It was a dense jungle trail and dropped kind of slightly into like a hollow and we decided this was where we wanted to set up our ambush. So when we got there, three of us was setting up the Claymore mines and the other two were standing security and you would put these Claymores just in the shape of an "L" about fifteen to twenty meters apart and after we had them set up -your Claymores are about six inches high and about ten inches wide, about an inch thick. It's got a steel quarter spring wound up inside of it and it's notched and when those things explode, all those notches disintegrate and they send out BBs and it's detonated by a blasting cap.

Well, after we got them in place and camouflaged we got back to the area behind the Claymores out of the backlash zone and we set up watch. Sometimes you got to wait a long time, days probably, before anything might happen and other times it just, everything happens real fast. We were up from about eight o'clock in the morning till about noon and about that time we -one of our men spotted five, they were Vietcong. They were local and judging that by their uniforms. They were coming down the trail and there was an area which was called the killing zone of these Claymores. After these guys got within the killing zone, we busted the caps on them. Exploded the Claymores. After the dust and everything cleared away, two of them were killed instantly and the other three were wounded badly and laying in the dirt, so we called back to our headquarters and told them what had happened and told them that three of them were still alive feeling that they might want them medivaced back and patched up and questioned. Well, they came back on the radio, that they didn't need any prisoners at that time and they told us to eliminate them. This wasn't an isolated incident. It happened to other details before, but it was the first time it ever happened to me and I didn't really know how to cope with it at the time.

I feel, you know, if it ever comes in a battle, just shoot them and let them -that would be it. There's a difference, I guess, when they call back and they tell you individually to take care of it or your team to take care of it. Anyway, we done what we supposed to do. We shot them and in this same area that we were put in for this ambush, just a few weeks before that a whole village of Montinyards was wiped out because they refused to give these local forces food and their young men to serve on their forces and that's why we were running a mission in that particular area.

PRETTY SLEEK

I know most of the guys in here were telling stories abut what went out in Vietnam, but I was never in the _____ outfit to tell you what went on but I can tell you what went on in the background. I was stationed with the 69th Signal Battalion and we were stationed on Tan San Hut Air Base and well, we supplied teletype communications for MACV headquarters and I must say we had it pretty _____ over there. We didn't get under fire. Well, as a matter of fact, I never had a rifle in my hand except once and then they didn't give me any bullets to put in it so you can tell by that, the war only got to Saigon once and that was in January the year before I got there and we used to ride a big school bus to work. It was about three miles from where we were compounded and the MACV headquarters. It was a pretty nice place. There was all prefab buildings with air conditioning and hot and cold running water. I know a lot of guys over there never had running water. I know a lot of guys over there never had it the whole time they were there, but we had two or three snack bars in that building. We'd go down and have a T-bone steak if we wanted it. About anything we wanted, in that snack bar you could have grilled ham and cheese or an egg omelet or something like that and the – most of the officers over there – I know Abrams and I forget the other dude, Westmoreland, I guess was his name, they had a two story apartment house for him and he was the only guy that lived there.

It was right there on the MACV compound and most of the other officers of that military systems command lived downtown in old French villas. They'd shack up with the civilian secretaries or people there. I don't know whether any of the guys knew about it – there was quite a few American secretaries who were in Vietnam working at MACV and they had – I think there was about three movie theaters over there, showing all the top-run movies you could go to. You could go to three different movies a week if you wanted to. There must have been four PXs around that area. They had one huge PX on Tan Sanh Hut Air Base that you could buy anything in that place. You could buy furs. You could buy tape recorders, set ups, everything. They had one bowling alley, which I forget how many lanes was in it. We used to go down there every once in a while.

Life at MACV it was pretty sleek and the thing I'm trying to get at is how anybody that's living under these conditions could ever run a war for guys who were stuck out in the middle of nowhere. The only thing that they have to go by is their intelligence and what they get from those men who were out in the field, but without that actual experience of what is going on, there's no way they can place theirselves in these men's shoes.

I FOUND OUT

I was stationed in U Dorn, Thailand, where there wasn't too much going on other than droppin' bombs or loading the bombs and sending them up north, but we had a lot of guys gettin' killed over in Thailand for some reason and after I got over there I found out why. The salary we were making in the States wasn't that much but over there it seemed like a lot of money because you could buy a lot with what you made and we used to go downtown on these _____ buses, which was a _____ with everybody sittin' on the back of it and what would happen over there, the Thai people knew when payday was and when you went downtown they would try to rob you and if you didn't fork over, they would kill you.

I had this one friend, a master sergeant, who was in our outfit and he had bought a gold four season bracelet. One night he was in a bar. These guys come over and they told him. Hey, give us your bracelet and he goes, oh, come on you guys, you're joking. Come on, I'll buy you a beer and forget it. Well they weren't joking. They pulled out a gun and shot him three times and then they ran like hell because they were pretty close to base and somehow he got back to the base and to the hospital and he survived all right and kept his bracelet, too, but that happened to a lot of guys. I know one major got knocked off like that and quite a few guys got run over by taxi-cabs over there. That's about all.

NO TRAINING

I was in the United States Air Force from 1962 to 1966. I spent four years in the United States, too. I didn't go overseas but I was with a Radar Bomb Squadron down in Georgia and our basic job was to compute bomb runs and see how accurate they were and in 1965 – in that area – they called one of our teams over, surveying teams – sent them to Vietnam to go over and survey that specific area and they had no training whatsoever as far as ground training or rifle training or anything of that nature for their own protection and they went over to Vietnam and they got out in the field and they had like two or three Army and Marine personnel that did have combat training and they was out one day and got wiped out. There was a team of about twelve surveyors. Not a one of them came back alive. But they did ship their bodies back in closed caskets and we had the funerals in the United States for each individual that was killed over there, and they all received medals.

Our unit received a citation and we just, from that experience alone, you could see how bad and how poorly trained some of our units were, how badly prepared they were to go into certain actions which I'm kind of glad myself I didn't have to go over. Although I did volunteer to go, I was never called. That's my experience.

IN THE OCEAN

I spent over twenty years in the service and Vietnam – that was a political war. I worked on various bombers and various tankers throughout my career in the service. In Vietnam, we would take our bombers, go out and bomb the targets predetermined by the politicians of both countries. We'd either go out and bomb non-essential targets or drop them in the ocean. We'd take our tankers and go out and dump fuel that was needed here in the States. Nine times out of ten, we'd dump our fuel because there was no bomber even set up to receive fuel and during the end of the war, I was sent to two different bases near Vietnam where we had over five hundred tankers at these two bases. We'd re-fuel to sixty to seventy thousand pounds of fuel for each tanker, fly thirty minutes, dump it and come back in. When the president finally said we could hit any place in Vietnam we wanted to, the war ended in five days. That's all I got.

THEY REALLY FEEL DEEP

When I was in the Army, it seemed like I never really heard anyone talk about being in Vietnam and I know there were a lot of men that were over there, but they just never seemed to talk about it. But I noticed in this class when a lot of the men talked about it, it really affected them, being over there, because you can really tell it affected them in some way, even though they tell joking stories sometimes and that, but they really feel deep that over there was really a life taking situation. That's all I have to say.

AN ACQUAINTANCE

I'll tell you a story about the time I was in base camp. I was working in the parts room at the time. I had only been in 'Nam about two months. It was the first part of January of '70 and I was back in the parts room and we had from time to time other guys come up to requisition parts and pick up parts and this one time I looked up and two guys were standing there at the outside window and I recognized one of them. So I stood up and when I stood up he recognized me. He wasn't what you would call a buddy, I guess, but an acquaintance from high school. So I went over and his name didn't ring right away when I saw him but I looked at him and he called me by name and when he did that rung a bell and I knowed him. Joe Antonelli was his name and got to bullshittin' with him.

Found out he was on a MACV searchlight team. So he told me he was going out that night on a mission, just around the perimeter with the searchlight team and wanted to know if I could go with him and continue our bullshit stories. So I told him I'd ask my C.O. and went down and I saw the C.O. The C.O. told me not tonight he couldn't let me go, but maybe the following weekend or the weekend after that he'd give me some time off. So I went back and I told Joe what the C.O. said. So we bullshitted another half hour or so. When Joe left it was getting near evening. We went down, finished work that day and went back down to the hootches and about midnight that night some of us guys was till up playing cards and bullshitting'. We heard taps being blowed and hearing taps being blown in 'Nam, was just about every night. But, I don't know, probably it's now that I think back about it or that it happened at the time, but I think I paid attention to the taps that night and you do, usually but that night special attention, but the next morning we held small formations, taking roll call and stuff; to make sure that nobody was missin'. Not a big formation, because you didn't want everybody grouped together in a combat zone.

So in formation, the captain come over, well, the sergeant called me out of formation and told me the captain wanted to see me. So I went down to the orderly room and the captain asked me if Antonelli was a buddy of mine. I told him, yeah, we went through high school. I think it was a grade and he told me that he was killed the previous evening. A rocket piercing grenade hit the jeep that they were on and from the remains of the jeep it must have hit dead center on the searchlight and he was operating the searchlight that night. It killed everybody in the jeep and the only thing that they found other than debris from the jeep was clothing and parts of limbs from the guys that were in it.

TO A TREE

I was stationed in U Dorn, Thailand, near Bangkok, Thailand, and I got there in the closing months of the war and I was in a special outfit – that we trained different countries, Laos, Cambodia, how to fight a war and how to fly the airplanes and load them and all the maintenance to it and we were there, you know. There were things we did, I guess, that were against the Geneva Convention or whatever it was because I remember when Jane Fonda went to Vietnam and they made a big stink over her being over there, then saying what she had said about the weapons or pictures that she used. I was a bomb loader and we handled all the equipment that was dropped or shot. We had – they used these one weapons where they were put in a package like, you know, a big bomb, when it was dropped it would tear apart and wouldn't per se explode, but it would drop these little balls and when these balls would reach a certain revolutionary speed, they would explode and what shot out of them was these, like little nails with like feathers on it except they were made out of metal and they'd shoot right into a human, you know, stick him to a tree or something and then they had something similar to it, again in a little ball. They were like little BBs and of course, we had rockets over there, little rockets and they were high explosives and white phosphorous and white phosphorous I'm pretty sure was against the Geneva Convention because it would burn you.

Burn the shit out of you, you know, just get it on you and just eats it's way through and like I said, we trained the Laotians and Cambodians and at the time there was a special detachment in the Air Force under the Army which was also under Air America which was supposedly under the C.I.A. but checking on that's pretty hard to do and during the time we were training Laotians, there was a coalition government of communists and the Laotian government theirself and also at the same time, we was training the Cambodians they were at war with, not the Viet Cong, but with the communists, you know, _____, I think the name of it was and we were trying to train them so that the faster we'd train them they'd go back and you know, and do their job but they eventually lost the war and most of the G.I.'s over there – drugs were pretty high, you know, pretty available.

You could go out and pick your own grass or whatever you wanted to and you'd be out there loading a bomb and your crew chief would be higher than hell, you know, and he'd be loading rockets into tubes. We had a couple of incidents, whether it was from drugs or whatever, you know, which had happened and like one time the crew chief threw the missile into the launcher and it went all the way through and went down to take the pins out so that you take off and fly and dropped the bombs and the bombs went right there on the ground and, so, you know, drugs are pretty available.

Before I got there, before the government really started their cracking down on drugs, they said they used to just get higher than hell, then go out and work with us, you know, pretty hectic for a pilot. They'd go out there and you know, a plane be screwed up and that's it for them. Our government-the American government used to give parties for the Laotians and Cambodian workers, their generals and so on and so on and it was funny because the Americans always got invited to the parties. It was never our party, you know, a party for us, when they threw a party it was always for them. They'd spend a couple of thousand bucks on whiskey and food and, you know, then just invite the American G.I's to their own party and all of that had – life over there was pretty good. We lived in huts, some of them had rooms, some of them didn't and the black market over there is pretty big. You can buy just about anything you wanted, stereos, jewelry, drugs, whatever you wanted to buy. A lot of whores downtown, you know, you can go to any bar and get laid. They had massage parlors every place. Everything was real cheap and a lot of guys threw their money away on that shit. That's all.

DISEASE

I got a story to tell. When we was overseas one time, we got a call to come back to stateside to fly an _____ back so it was just on the spur of the moment, you know, this happened. We get on the plane and we come stateside. Well, hell, all these guys, you know, was on the beach and everything. We had this one guy. We picked him up off another crew. He was _____. See when they caught him he was off on the beach some damn place and we got him and just flying stateside and they called him -the plane called in and told all those guys wives and stuff to meet them. You know what I mean. Hell, we'd been out of the states for six months. So, well, I learned his first name. His first name was Larry and oh, he was worried because his wife would be there to meet him, you know, and he said, hell, I don't want to go to bed with her or nothing, but anyway he gets there.

They go home that night, I guess, you know, and I guess, you know what the hell, he's going to screw her, you know. They've been gone that long so anyway two, three days later, you know, he starts bitchin', raising hell at her, you know, and said something about he caught some kind of God-damned disease off of her. So anyway, here comes to find out she was screwing on him, you know while he was gone. Yeah. That's no bullshit, but he didn't think anything about it. You know, he was trying to plant it on her, you know what I mean so she didn't throw it back at him and by God, you know, she really screwed around him while he was -he had something, so did she. She'd of died if he give it to her.

FOR A FACT

(tape begins in middle of story)

What'd they call any of this stuff or anything else. I'd heard rumors, you know, in an island off the coast they sent all these incurables to, but now whether they really did that, I don't know. I guess you had to have it before you really found out, but I know one guy that there wasn't no fooling about that. I know it for a fact. That was around Christmas time in '66. He got a dose and sometimes separated, sometimes together and because _____. Found out anyway and it was in, hell, May or June, I think the next time I really got to talk to him and, hell, he was still going to the doctor twice a day and he hadn't gotten rid of it yet. As to what happened to him, whether he came back home when the rest of us did or not, I don't know. That's why in the United States, venereal disease is a problem but over there it was really more serious. It's been there longer and the stronger the strain of it, the longer it takes to get rid of it. I think in Asia they've got one of the few strains of syphilis that even the early stages can't even be arrested and I always heard that they sent them to an army hospital in Japan. It was like a city. It was guarded like a small city within Japan somewhere. It was like guarded by the military. You couldn't come out and just workers could come in and that's where they'd send soldiers that got incurable syphilis and so forth and different diseases.

Comment: Did they just stay there until it went to the brain and killed them?

Yeah. It's just a matter of time before it wipes them out. It, well they say if you get it like if you're a teenager, eighteen or nineteen and if you never have anything done to you, by thirty-eight it will eat your brain up.

Comment: WE had a guy that over in 'Nam he had it for six years and he came back over to Thailand when he was there and he still had trouble with the dripping and stuff and they cut his dick open and they still couldn't cure it and they didn't – they just sent him back to the States. They didn't do anything special to him.

They always said, you know, if you catch the clap, gonorrhea after so many times, it will make you sterile. Well, I had it thirteen times when I was over there. I've got four kids and they all seem to be healthy.

Comment: I think half the war was diseases.

When I came back to the States and every time I go for a physical, like, well, I went to take a mine physical one time. Dr. _____ was giving it to me and I told him about all those different times I had gonorrhea and I told him I'd like to have my blood tested for any venereal type disease and every time I go get a physical, I tell them the same thing. They do it and they tell you the results.

Comment: In case of a relapse maybe. You're lucky. They always said, you now, that – hell, that gonorrhea won't come back but I've _____. Well, I just don't want to take the chance. Well, the only thing I can say about it is it's fun while you're getting it, but it's hell to get rid of.

A WHITE AND BLACK

This happened between a white and black. The black was the one that got _____ and he come walking back in the area with his duffle bag and this one guy told him, he says, you'll never spend another night in here alive. So as soon as he came back in with his duffle bag, he packed the rest of his gear and he was back out on the road going back to the division so he wasn't staying there because, you know, the threat to life and whenever that happened, nobody would come down on him either. Like you'd go to the department and say, hey, this guy in this unit swears he's going to get me. I'm not staying here another night. They don't let you go back until they could make arrangements for you to go to another unit because that happened. I seen it happen.

A LITTLE HOOTCH

In 1969, we were on one of those good turns of liberty in Sasimo, Japan. Our sister squadron had a gang of fellows down on the beach somewhere near the Japanese-American Embassy and they were engaged in a softball game. Apparently, they had a lot of booze and most of them, I guess, got pretty drunk to where they didn't even know what they were doing. Some of the men involved were senior enlisted men of this squadron. In fact, one man was the senior most enlisted man of the entire squadron. These fellows, decided, after the ballgame that they would climb the flagpole and steal the Japanese flag. Well, this didn't go over too big. In fact, it really created an international incident and this particular E-9 Chief was without question cross-decked to another carrier, to another squadron, which he didn't see the States for some time to come. Some of the other fellows were transferred. A few were busted. The whole moral, I guess, of the story is it just shows you what a few fellows can do when they get hold of a little hootch.

DON'T...

Well, this was when I just come back from Vietnam. My brother-in-law was right up on the flight line and I went up to see him. We were both sergeants and I went up to see him and I had some grease on my finger and I asked for a rag and I was wiping my hand off and there was a T-38, state side(A-38 in Vietnam). I laid the rag down and about that time he said, "Don't lay it..." and they started to lift the engines off and it sucked it right in there. Boy. I don't know how much damage it caused but it really messed that up.

A SHARPSHOOTER

Another time down in Long Kou, we was on guard duty and we all got high on – we had a couple of fifths and we all got high and a mamasan was out in a rice paddy with her water buffalo and normally, the custom is, the women usually handle the water buffalo for some odd reason. The men can't handle them, but they have a ring in their nose and she just leads it along by the ring and one of the guys, you know, he was a sharpshooter. He was pretty good with a gun. Even though he was high, he still managed to denut the bull, you know.

CHANGING THE NUMBERS

I never had too much, well I never had anything to do, I suppose, with Vietnam. I was in the service at that time. I was with a patrol outfit huntin' Russian U-boats, submarines. We just more or less watched and whatever they got into, we were supposed to report, I guess. I spent most of my time in the North Atlantic, the Mediterranean and the Azores and I know one time when I was in the Med., we was in for about twelve months. We kept getting calls on patrol that a bunch of Russian U-boats – they counted at least sixty or seventy in the Mediterranean. They wanted to know what they was doing and we had to chase them and find out – we had a hard time finding them. We'd find a few here and a few there but you could never learn how they went down – maybe sixty or seventy in there.

So about six months later, we was flying around the damn coast there and we seen god-damned U-boats docked up in one of these coves and we come down low about forty foot toward the top of them. There they got the sons-of-a-bitches out there chipping paint off and changing the numbers on those son-of-bitch boats. There was just about two or three boats in there and them bastards were changing numbers all the time and we spent somewhere around twelve months huntin' them and while I was up there, they caught the Pueblo, when I was stationed – I think I was in the Azores at that time, I'm not sure and I think we was in Iceland for a fuel-up after that and they had everything – we took over for the army.

I got extended while I was there because they said something about I'd be in for the duration. I didn't know what the hell that meant. I had to go ask. They told me if war broke out I was in there first. If the war lasted from now until doomsday, that's how long I had to stay in the service, but we never did get called out on that. We were up close. They had interceptors all lined up to take off on that but nothing ever happened.

WHAT WE ARE

What I'd like to say is that Vietnam, if that didn't do anything else, I think it hooked a lot of the people up in the United States as to what the American soldier really was. Up until then they'd always had a picture of being Johnny Next Door. Mr. Nice Guy. Chivalrous in battle and all that bull, but they hung Calley or tried to hang him for doing what he was told to do, to begin with for something that happened every damn day. They just pulled him out of all them and decided well, we'll crucify this bastard., but if nothing else, that's one thing everyone have found out about 'Nam or should know about 'Nam. That probably one of the meanest, cruelest bastard guys that ever walked the earth is an American G.I.

I mean if you'd read in the paper about somebody being in a hole about two feet wide, three feet long and two feet deep covered with barbed wire and someone said it was an American G.I., oh, that would be a terrible thing to do to him. What kind of inhuman animal would do that to a person? Well, the guy that I saw in that hole wasn't an American G.I. It was a Vietcong because he wouldn't talk they put him in a hole. He couldn't stretch out. He couldn't set up. He couldn't stand up. The only thing he could do was lay there all humped up and he lay for twenty-four hours that I know of before they ever decided to let him out of it and as far as Calley running in and shooting up a village of people and killing as many as they say he did, well, he – no way he was all by himself pulling that stuff like that because I've been in raids on villages where there was no prior warning. No nothing else. As far as we knew, there wasn't even any soldiers in the damn village.

Just pull up on a hill over top the damn thing and blow it away, but if we're going to have any more wars, let's at least be realistic about it. Let's not try to play Mr. Nice Guy. Let's let everyone know exactly what we are.

SHAKE HANDS

Well, the way the United States built up these prisoners and more or less made war heroes out of them, when actually I feel that these soldiers that were captured for such a long period over there they are probably actually ashamed, you know, to face anybody. Let alone I don't know how many millions of people over the United States watched them board off of that plane and shake hands with a full bird, general, or whatever the hell he was. I think when a man's captured overseas he's pretty well lost enough pride that by bringing him back and facing the people of the United States it probably killed every little bit of integrity or pride that he might have left inside of him along with the idea of all the hell and torment he went through over the three, four, five, or six years he might have been captured. That's all.

AN OLD LADY

About the only time we got a chance to go out in the field was after we got separated from the mission we was in Vietnam. The first American that I got to see, well, they showed us movies before we went over to Vietnam and the first American soldier I ever saw really murdered like this. He had his hands bound behind his back and his head was amputated and they had a hell of a time finding his dog tags. Then they go ahead and a couple of guys he was with, they went ahead and tied one of those tags around his foot, you know, and then they laid a bag beside him. I guess they'd go ahead and have somebody pick him up. But we went to a village and the lieutenant that was with us, he had his handgun, of course, and one of the guys shot an old lady and he was calling for a medic and the lieutenant took him over and told him, "Don't call for a medic." He said, "Go on." Well, as soon as we moved out towards the other end of the village, we heard a shot and then the lieutenant come walking behind us. We knew what he did. He shot her, you know, put her out of her misery. They didn't let the medic come in and, you know, take care of her.

GOLD

In 1975 when I was stationed in Fort Meade, Maryland, I was with the 72nd Medical Battalion and we got a call that we had to leave, so we went to Guam. I was over there seventy-three days and at the time, they were bringing the Vietnamese by boat from Vietnam, screening them to come to the United States and at the time I met three or four different people that brought back gold, American currency, that they couldn't have gotten unless they got it through the black market, totaling approximately one to two million dollars per person. Most of them came – they bought their way over because at the time they were bringing them over they brought them over by different groups. Most of the people came over by Air Force planes – these people they came over by American, United Airlines, and other famous airlines. There were a lot of people that were sick and they had to stay there for thirty, forty, fifty days. They only operated on two sides of the island. We were on the north side and the southern side was operated by another battalion. The monsoons hit about the last fifteen to twenty days we were there and it made it all the worse because they were keeping on bringing them in and we had to keep them there because a lot of people were too sick to leave at the time they were supposed to and that's all.

OVER IN GREECE

We come back from Vietnam in '70 and then they had us go on a cruise in the Mediterranean Sea because of the Turkey uprisings. So we was over in Greece, had our base set up and this one guy he was all the time getting in trouble. He was smoking dope and marijuana and everything. So this one night, you know, he's on speed so about four or five of them all got a sheep and you know, tried to make love to a sheep and the M.P.s got them and made them –put them in jail. The next night they was on guard duty. They stole the shotguns from, you know, they was walking guard and had shotguns so they took the shotgun and went down and stole the water truck and about seven of them jumped on it and took off into this little town and they came to this one, like – a whiskey store. So they broke into the store and stole all the whiskey and the Greek officials came and they shot at him with a shotgun. They took off in the water truck in the other direction. They didn't want to face them and they got in the water truck, come back and ran into about two or three of the tents that was set up and killed I don't know how many chickens, dogs enroute back to our base. In order to get back, you know, from the officials from Greece. That's about it.

In 1962

In 1962 I was in _____ France and we had naval exercises come up and we went up to one of those secret bases in a place called _____. It was up near the Luxembourg border, right above Nancy and the base was so well camouflaged that I had my _____set up in _____ so he'd water almost a week on this ground before I knew I was on the roof of a building. It was really well camouflaged. The buildings were big cement structures, real cold. We got there in August. It was like in the midst of this forest there. You couldn't see anything. You couldn't even tell the buildings were there. Grass on the roof, the whole bit and the water supply up there was pretty terrible so the French brought a hundred cases of white and a hundred cases of red wine in. The Germans brought in a couple of hundred cases of beer so we didn't drink too much water all the time we were up there.

The thing that came out of these exercises, in 1962, Der Spiegel magazine got a hold of the reports of these exercises and the German minister of defense and it almost caused Konrad Adenaur and Lloyd Brum to resign. If that had happened, if they had resigned, they would have had a different German president over there. But a lot of this secret information came out of that.

A ROBBERY

I was in Vietnam from May of '67 to May of '68. I spent about the first three months in the field and I got stationed in Saigon about a month before the Tet Offensive and at the time I was there, there was a robbery. When you come in country, you turn your American currency into MPC and all the money stays right in the country because they have a big turnover and when you leave, you just change your MPC back into American currency again. There was twenty-six people involved in this robbery and they estimated it took close to three years for the robbery to go through and the highest ranking official was a major that was involved with it and all the way down to a private E-2. When they found this out, they had twenty-six people and two or three of the people was already out of the service and there was about six left in country. The others was still in the service and stationed indifferent parts of the United States and Europe. They took them all back to Vietnam and they had a trial and I was a guard over an E-6 -staff sergeant and they had the trials, there was I think four or five of them that pleaded guilty and they got a sentence of a year. The rest of them pleaded not guilty and all but one got sentenced but the general in charge, he lessened their sentences. Cut it in half. But everyone that was involved in that robbery, they got all the money out of the country. There wasn't no way they could find out where it was at or anything like this. They had the Internal Revenue Service stay on it the whole time. They're probably still on it. The E-6, he admitted afterwards that he probably got most of the money out, close to two million dollars and he was the only one that got away free.

A MISTAKE

When I first went over in 'Nam in '69 I was in Da Nang, the Eleventh Motor Transport. I was there for about fifteen days so we all woke up this morning. All of a sudden the sky was black, powder coming all over the compound and all of a sudden everybody was scared. There was sirens going off. We didn't know what was going on. Here the ASP-1 Ammo Dump, it blew up, and it blew up all the bombs that they had. Really it was just a mistake of the guy that cleaned. He set a fire and it just set the whole – exploded. The whole ammo dump was on fire and they wasted, I forget how many tons of ammunition which could have been prevented. But no, this guy was burning garbage right beside the compound where they kept the explosives and right there in Da Nang next to the airstrip. The people were scared in a little town there so they sent us all out in convoys to, you know, evacuate all the people. All because of that guy's mistake.

ANYTHING THAT MOVES

We was in Da Nang and we just was flying there from _____, Thailand and we was there for three nights and when you are in transit like that and Da Nang was known as a rocket city. Because they, well, I think from '66 all the way during the end of the war they were shelled every night and it was no small base there. I mean it was fairly large. I think they housed something like close to 30,000 and then I think besides it and Plei Ku, I think it was about the third biggest base in Vietnam, but we was out there. We was sleepin' and they hit the flight line that night so when they rang the alarm, my job was to go – we had a pre-arranged post to go to and at the time we went out there, it started raining and our business, I mean they said shoot at anything that moves. Well, it was one of those nights where you can't see the fight line. It just seems like you can see silhouettes or anything moving, the trees and everything and just like a silhouette type thing.

I was laying in like a ditch. It was like a bunker type thing but it was almost like a ditch and I shot at about anything that moved. I mean I really emptied the rifle out, you know, and I figured – I estimated myself on being a good shot and that night, I think maybe I just shot a little crazier than I would any other time. But I remember seeing a person running and I shot and they went down and that was almost morning and by that time the rain stopped but I was laying in about six to eight inches – it was even with my back – the water was. I was cold. I was – I didn't know how cold it was until the next day, but I was scared more than anything and when after all the shellin' and everything stopped, the mortar attacks and the firing, we were supposed to go out to the edge of the flight line and I guess, check the perimeter or whatever, but it seems like my one – when I saw that person fall, that's the first person I ever, you know, that I believe I ever shot in Vietnam and I looked left and right, but my point of vision always seemed to come back center to that one area and I walked up and it's hard to tell how old. It was a boy that I shot – I hit in the shoulder and he was carrying gun belts and he was carrying what they call their sand box grenades. He had them on his belt and evidently he was carrying for a father and uncle or whatever. But it didn't bother me, seeing that so much as it did seeing, you know I knew that I killed him but it didn't bother me so much as seeing the guy that might have been lying next to me that all night screamed for a medic and the medic didn't get to him for maybe an hour or two later.

It wasn't a type of thing where these people weren't sharpshooters. They were expert at guerrilla warfare. They could make mortars. They would make a mound out of dirt, take a tube, put a mortar in it, put three or four logs behind it and set a fuse to it and they would go, I believe they would be a half mile to a mile away when the rockets left, you know, when they were fired and they might go helter skelter, but one hits. That's their main objective and when you went out to check, to see what happened, they were gone. They were long gone. Like I said, we were in a base war. We weren't allowed to go behind the fence. We were allowed to look, but we weren't allowed to touch.

MONSOONS

Okay, I'd like to talk about when I was living in the field. Base camp was right beside _____. It was between Phan Rang and Cam Ranh Bay and in the MACV compound. They were the headquarters for the ARVN soldiers and the Vietnamese army and before our compound had moved, we were Combat Engineers and it was like a valley, a dried river bed, see, and the captain of the MACV had told us that in the monsoons it floods the river and the commanding officer says, "Oh well, it'll not wash us out. We won't be here that long."

So the first monsoons come. I think it rained, the first day it rained well, three days straight in a row and the water started risin' and they had everybody off work details and buildin' sand bags. Sand baggin' up the river. I think there was one tent that only had something like eighteen inches of water. The rest of them was just completely full and washed away. And so the army let us – I don't know why they did it – I don't see how they was responsible – they let us claim all our personal stuff that we had lost, see, and they had no way of proving it. Well, I think the first time I lost a pair of civilian shoes and I claimed $580.00 worth of stereos, cameras, and stuff like that and so that was over and we come back and cleaned up the compound and got ready for military business again.

So here about two weeks, two and one half weeks later, here comes some more rain and it was real, real heavy and we were right in this valley. So to prepare for it, we moved down the road, got a Bailey Bridge, tore it down, took it back, put it up because it was higher than – we had an old rope bridge, it washed away. So the second time, the commanding officer didn't listen. He was bound and determined, you know, because he built him a great big command post. I think it was about, oh, fifty, sixty feet high. This one Red Cross girl, doughnut girl, they crashed into it once. It killed them, because they had no light on the top and so the second flood came and it just took everything. I mean, well, they had to come and get us with LARKS, you know, amphibious boats from Cam Ranh Bay, and here we was, no ammunition, no guns. The river just took them all away. So we come back the next – well, they shipped us out to different companies. Then we come back about a week later and the water had gone down and everything. I think there was scorpions all over the place and bamboo – just – we had to clean it up. That's just how stupid the army was.

This shows how ignorant these people are. You know, I mean, not ignorant. They're smart if they want to be smart, but they just didn't care. So one time this village we were by, somewhere the Red Cross or somebody had got together and got them something like five thousands bushels of soybeans to take to the village and to replant and to build up their agriculture and stuff and so here the MACV supervisor goes down two weeks later to see how much they had got planted and cultivated and all they did was just ate them. They just ate the beans and said to hell with it.

COUPLE OF SHACK JOBS

I was stationed up at Griffith Air Force Base and we had this group of KC-135s flying through there and they had all tight security. You couldn't get down the runway near the planes and all that stuff and then a couple of master sergeants went down to the Brass Rail in Rome and decided to get drunk and they were down there talking about going back to California. They were stationed at March Air Force Base and a couple of local girls there, they hung around the bar, decided they wanted to go to California, so the two master sergeants were pretty well on their way and they figured that would be a chance to line up a couple of shack jobs back there in California with them – take them back with them.

So they smuggled them on board, went down through the flight line. That's how good the security was. Got them on board the KC-135, stowed them away. They loaded up, re-fueled and everything, had the planes ready to go, got up in the air, made an in-flight inspection, discovered the girls after they were in the air for about fifteen minutes and they had to fly those KC-135s as a group all the way back to Denver, Colorado. There was, I think, six or seven of them. Bring them back to Rome, New York. They had to get rid of some of the fuel load, to make a landing and I think it cost in excess of something like eight thousand dollars per plane to bring those girls back.

The Inspector General called me up. I was working night cook that night and he says, asked, you know, if they bring some people up to feed them so they brought them up. They had FBI, IG, OSI, all the plane pilots and they were bitchin' and moanin' because from then on they had to stand guard on their own planes. Of course, the two master sergeants, one of them had 19 years and the other one had 17 years, both of them got kicked out with dishonorable discharges and some jail time. The two girls got off with three to five years probation.

WANTED TO GO

I have a story about a man I was in the service with at one time. He decided he'd like to go to Vietnam, you know. He wanted to go. I was in the Navy at Norfolk and he wanted to go to Vietnam and he finally finagled his way around. He finally got orders to go and he got orders to go on a riverboat. He wanted to shoot a machine gun. That was his big thrill in life. He wanted to wear cross-bandoliers across himself, you know, and he actually sent a picture back. He was standing there and had machine gun belts or whatever around him. He really thought he was something. I heard later about three months after he had that picture taken that he got killed and I was just, you know, wondering what a waste it was because he would never have had to have went, you know, if he didn't really want to. I mean he just wanted to go so bad and then he got killed.

MAJOR GOT PROMOTED

I was in the First Division in Vietnam and we was a mobile outfit and there were all the doctors and nurses, had a real field hospital in a place called _____ outside of Saigon and we had a major who was the head of the battalion and he wasn't a doctor and if you're in a mobile outfit, unless you are a doctor, you get no rank. They just pass over you and he had about five years in rank and he wanted promoted bad, as if he could taste it. So he came up with this bullshit that when the men go out on patrols they are to carry no weapons. He said there is to be no weapons so we did this for about three months and after some hell raising, orders came down that we could carry 45's so then he got another bright idea – that medics would go out on convoys as drivers. So after some more hell raisin' that got changed. He still didn't get promoted, so he said, "Well, I got another brainstorm."

Near there was a town and the Air Force built a school, so he said, "I'm going to volunteer to build a school for these people because they need it." So we all volunteered to build the school. All the generals were there and the Stars and Stripes photographer was there for the dedication and one of the sergeants and he got wasted by one of the villagers and of course, it was a big hush. They changed the name of the school, from the sergeant's name and the Major got promoted to a colonel.

Wess: That was after he was dead?

Yeah.

PEOPLE TOLD ME

During the war in Vietnam I was stationed in Germany. In the biggest part of the war I was in a tactical helicopter company and I never really thought much about Vietnam except for what the people told me, pilots and all and most of them when they – they'd tell stories about _____ babies in the war with (indistinguishable). Things like that. It really sickens you. I'm glad as hell I never went there.

MOLE HOLE

Okay, I'm number three and what I have to say doesn't have anything to do with the war itself because during the war period I was still in high school, but the same summer or spring that we pulled out of 'Nam I graduated from high school and volunteered for active duty in the Air Force. Well, I went through the basic training and the job I went into – they didn't have to give me a tech school so I went directly to the base I was assigned to after a ten day leave to start my job, on-the-job training.

The base I went to was in North Carolina near the east coast. It was mainly a Tactical Air Command base with also Strategic Air Command squadrons on it and after I'd been there for a while I got put on the night shift crew of the motor pool where I worked and all we did all night long was take buses with crews for B-52's and KC-135's back and forth from their planes for making the trips – the base hops – where they would file their flight plans and missions. All this was sort of prevention type stuff for any after-effects of what might come from the war, I guess. We had one spot on the base itself, what we all referred to as the "mole hole." What this was, was a building of about three stories built underground on one far end of the base where they kept one squadron of B-52's and one squadron of KC-135's refueled, manned and ready to go at all times. This mole hole was like a combination of barracks, cafeteria and necessity facilities and the flight crews and anybody that had anything to do with those planes would live in it at all times.

They would stay there for three weeks at a time without being able to leave and then they would be off duty for another three weeks or something like that and you couldn't even get near that building unless you had a secret clearance or higher and being a driver, I had to have at least a secret clearance for hauling food back and forth and supplies and this was, you know, defensive type stuff all the time that they always had to be ready to be off the ground within a couple of minutes in case of any type of disaster or emergency and along with those B-52's and tankers, we had four squadrons of F-4 Phantom fighters that were in there.

There was never a minute that went by that you didn't see one fly around or you didn't hear them firing up their engines or testing the engines to make sure that everything was in A-1 shape, ready to go and the main thing that bugged me when I first got there was the fact you would go to bed at night or whenever and try to go to sleep and all you hear was these jet engines roaring in your ear, twenty-four hours a day and it seemed like a lot of times it was just for no good reason, wasting a lot of fuel and a lot of taxpayer's money for things that wasn't being used at the time.

FIRST LOOK

I'll tell you a little bit about what I thought about 'Nam when I first arrived. I was shipped to Fort Lewis, Washington with orders to go to 'Nam. We were there three days. It was a hassle, everybody scared to death. We did leave one morning, which was on the first of November. We left, went through Hawaii, had a four hour layover in Hawaii, left there, stopped at Guam, left Guam with great anticipation, landed in 'Nam at Cam Ranh Bay. The first thing that caught my attention when the doors opened is the smell. All of 'Nam smells the same way. It stinks. The smell is rotten. The air is rotten. The soil is rotten and the next thing I noticed when I stepped out of the plane was the humidity. It was hot. It was at night when we got there. They took us down for orientation and we left there and we was in holding, I believe for three days and during that three days you find out what thirst is like.

I don't know if we were an exception or the rule but they had no water bags up and the only place you could get a drink was down at one of the clubs and me being a young kid, I was, I didn't take no money with me. I spent it all at Fort Lewis and nobody there – you're not going to see anybody once you get shipped out, so nobody's going to lend you any money so you find out what thirst is like and that was my first look at 'Nam.

WHAT IT DID

I was in the Navy from 1967 to 1971 and I never left the United States which I think I was kind of lucky. A lot of my friends went to Vietnam and I seen what it did to some of them and really, I never thought it was as bad as it was until, you know, I really saw what happened to them. I mean, some of them came back crippled and a lot of them never came back at all and which just, you know, it made me glad that I didn't have to go and really that's just about all I have to say about it.

HERO

My wife had a cousin that went to Vietnam when I was up in Rome, New York. He was nothing but a punk. He gets over there and he decides that the service wasn't for him so he goes AWOL and about six months later they found him – he was – well, they found his body. He was over there shacked up with one of those girls and I guess the V.C. caught him and of course, when they brought him back to the States, he was a big hero, all through there, upstate New York and of course his parents were glad to get the $10,000.00 plus back pay with which they purchased motorcycles and bought boats and a new car and within a year all these things were sold and they were back on welfare again, so that's how much he was worth.

CATTLE

I wasn't stationed in Vietnam. I enlisted in the Air Force. About the only thing I saw as a result of Vietnam was I got a hop out of Anchorage back to the lower forty-eight states in a hospital plane and all I got to say about it, it looked like a truckload of butchered cattle. Really sickening.

TECHNICAL INSPECTORS

I'm number twelve and I was in Vietnam from August 1971 to August 1972. I was in the 717th Air Cav. I was a gunner on a UH-1 chopper and at this particular time, we was working on our choppers and wherever they told us to go, we had to go. We couldn't take our maintenance men with us or our TI's (technical inspectors). Anyway, the crew chief and gunners(it would be one for performing maintenance) and like I say, we didn't have no technical inspectors and we was putting a short shaft in from the – just like a drive shaft connects to the transmission to the turbine engine – and after we got her all finished, they went for pre-flights. Well, the pilots got in and the crew chiefs and the gunners. Really, all of them wasn't supposed to get in there, but they got in anyway and they went up for a pre-flight and the short shaft came down in flight and they crashed and burned and got them all. That's all I have.

A DOSE

After I made my first cruise over to 'Nam, we came back to the States for a couple of years and then we went to the Med and I played on the ship's softball team and every time we came near a port or something, the whole team went over and played the locals a little game of softball. Well, this one time we'd been out to sea for about sixty days and most of us was pretty tired and ____ so the nine starters on the softball team started the game and there was about eight of us that weren't starters on the ball team and we slipped over to the local bar and into the girls' places. Yeah. It was in this particular town, I forget, Corfu, I think it was, Greece, and there really wasn't a town, just like an old farm village and houses and they was these prostitute houses, were these old farmhouses. Well, about two weeks later, it seemed like, eight guys on the softball team which hadn't been on liberty for two months come up with a dose of the clap. It kind of looked bad on us since we didn't show up for the ball game. Now, eight out of seventeen got the clap. That's all.

MAMASAN

Okay, when I was in _____, I went downtown and got to know this mamasan. She worked in the compound there and I had a friend of mine, well, we just go to be real good friends together and she invited me down and I went down there and got to know her real well. She was about eight months pregnant to one of the guys that already went home, one of the sergeants there, and I used to go down to visit her – got to visiting her quite a bit and taking my friends down there and then I ventured into stayin' all night and when I did, I took, I think a case of beer and everything and my buddy and I went down there and we set for a while and it got long towards curfew and he decided he was goin' to go back to the compound and I was gonna risk stayin' for the night and I went ahead and stayed and along about 10 o'clock, I guess it was, we started gettin' mortar fire to the company, from Charlie, and there was counter-fire comin' back and I was right in the middle of it and a little bit later, why somebody came knockin' at the door and she told me to just keep my mouth shut and I had nothin' to do with that rifle. I figured I'd be a lost cause where I was anyway, so I just trusted her to take care of everything and she went over to the door. I'll never know what she said, but she came back and I asked her who it was and she said Charlie and I tell you, I was shittin' and I thought, "Uh, oh, boy am I done" but she said that it's okay that they wouldn't bother me and yet today I don't know if it was the fact that I was a good Joe to the people or what, but I got away with that and when it was all said and done – the next morning – I stayed the night – the next morning I went to the compound and I never went back.

SHE JUST TOLD ME

I was in the Army a couple of years after the Vietnam war and was well – when the United States supposedly got out and I met a lot of people that were over there while I was in the service and some of them were female nurses. One of them was my roommate whenever I was going to nurse's training school and she worked on a Medivac unit and she evacuated a lot of guys and stuff like this and she just told me all kinds of stories that I didn't really believe but, you know, she just – through the experience – I had a captain that was over there and I mean, they really got kind of depressed whenever they told these stories about Vietnam and all that stuff. But you know, I just don't think that I would want to have anything to do with it. I wouldn't want to ever have to go through that.

SUPPORTIN' SHREVEPORT

I was stationed in Louisiana in the Air Force, a photo recon lab, so we really didn't have too much to do with the war effort. This base, at Shreveport, Barksdale, sort of had its heyday in the Cuban Missile Crisis, whenever that was and our mission there was making target maps for the Ukraine. There was another little top secret base tucked away inside of it where you had to have passes to get off and on and this was about 1970, I guess. We really didn't do anything there. We had all our jets on the flight line. We used to fire them up every night, but didn't go anywhere. And we run all our little exercises and had our little war games but I mean we weren't fighting, we were supportin' Shreveport. That was about it. They've closed most of the base down since then.

PRISONERS

Well, what I was going to talk about was when I got my orders to go overseas and my orders were to go to Italy. I thought that was kind of crazy at the time because I never volunteered for anything. My wife was pregnant and I wasn't too excited about going, but I thought I better take Italy rather than Vietnam. I was supposed to leave Laredo, Texas, four months after I got my orders and I think it was ten days after I got my orders they told me I was going to leave in a week.

They didn't tell me where I was going to go. They said I couldn't take my wife. My security clearance was changed from secret to top secret and I took off and went to Kennedy International Airport. From there, I was picked up by the Air Police and taken to McGuire Air Force Base in New Jersey where I was briefed for two days and from there, I was flown to _____ Air Base, Italy and we was shuttled from Italy to Germany, from Germany to Thailand, where we stayed there. I think we was there for almost a month and had our security clearance re-checked and we had our briefing to the area which we was going to. Our duty was to try to get some eighty to ninety prisoners of war out of a prisoner of war camp, under surveillance and everything. For the last month while we was in training, they watched different movement that the Vietnamese were moving the prisoners of war.

So the day we was supposed to go there, we went ahead and got in the choppers and everything. My job was I was a gunner in one of the pickup choppers. They had two on each side of the chopper and the prisoner of war camp was shaped like an oval shape. Three ships were supposed to go on, say, the left side of the base and they would drop men down who would in turn go across the perimeter of the camp and see how many men they could pick up or give their men cover to get out of the camp. Our job was to hover above the river and then come down in an opening and start picking them up. Well, these men, I think five of them, three Air Force and two Army, got out of the chopper. They went across the perimeter. The V.C. opened fire and there was nobody there. We went ahead and they told us to get the hell out and get out fast, so that's what we did.

It ended up that they estimated the men that was in the camp could have left maybe two to three hours before that time. There should have been somebody there. No one was hurt. I think they counted numerous casualties on the North Vietnamese side , but out of the five that went down on the ground, I think well, we all got the Air Medal but two got the Congressional Medal of Honor. I think it was during a football game they were awarded this. One Black Air Force Tech Sergeant and I think an Army Sergeant and all that training, all that was in vain, really for nothin'.

ESCALATION

I was part of President Johnson's "I don't believe in escalation, but send them 50,000 more." To me that war over there was not really a war. It was a big business money-making proposition in which this country did not fight like it would have in World War II. In World War II, we would have gone in and destroyed. A little country such as that is with the equipment that the opposition had over there we could have blew them off the maps and been out of there within a week with no trouble. In my opinion, this war was fought completely wrong and only for big business, with the dollars that they could make out of it. We didn't do anything but back out of there like cowards.

1049 FOR VIETNAM

I didn't go to Vietnam but I thought it was kind of funny the orientation that you go through in basic training and then when you go to your permanent party. The Army has a unique way of picking leaders for NCO's. They have good leaders but they have more bad than good. They drill you to where you're believing that you're going to end up in Vietnam and you may not. For instance, when I went in, a buddy of mine that I graduated from high school with and I went together and about half way through boot camp, they took us into a little room and tried to get us to re-up. Their pitch was, "Well, if you don't re-up, you'll probably end up as a "ground pounder" over in V.C. land, but if you re-up for three years, we'll give you a school. We'll send you to any school that you want to go to." Well, it sounded pretty good, you know, but I decided I'd take my chances.

My buddy took the three years. I came out of basic training and went to radio telephone radiac meter and teletype repairman. He come out of the school as a radio operator. He went to Germany and then to Vietnam and I stayed in the States. But what tickled me most of all was the fact that the NCO's kept telling you that this was the thing to do, put in a 1049 for Vietnam. The Department of the Army every month would send down requisitions for so many MOS's in job classifications and if your MOS was on that list then you had a pretty good chance of going to Vietnam. One month, approximately three months before I got out, the DA send down their list and about three-fourths of the MOS's that were on that list were E-6 and above slots. We had E-6's and above in our outfit. There were six of them that had anywhere from twelve to seventeen years in the service. These E-6's all put in retirement papers. They were gettin' out. They were not goin' to Vietnam.

BASIC

Okay, I'd like to talk about basic training for the women enlistees in the Army. Whenever I enlisted in the Army, I was under the impression that it was really going to be hard training and really out there in the field all the time. We went out there with all these weapons and learned how to run and to do this and do that and everything. Whenever, I got there it wasn't half as bad as what I expected. (....) We had classes on different field gear, such as anti-tank weapons and hand grenades and things like this, you know. We were just given classes on those, but we were taken to the range with an M-16 and out of a platoon – not a platoon – a company of three hundred girls, only about fifty of them qualified with an M-16 and I was one of them. Now, I just thought that I had to do it and I did and you know, whenever I first went in, I went in with the idea, well, you know, you're really going to make it or you're not and I made it through basic training because I knew that was what I really wanted to do and it was the first thing in life that I really achieved, that I really wanted to do. But I went in with the impression that it was going to be worse than it really was. It was really nothing.

NOT TRAINED

I'd like to start from the beginning when I got my draft papers and I had maybe three choices, either Canada, jail, or 'Nam, so I, being a loyal American, I went to 'Nam. The Army handled the situation so sloppy I thought that they rush you through basic training, through a couple of weeks of training and right straight into the fighting without really formal training. I was trained as a truck driver in AIT and was shipped to an infantry unit. The first four months I was there, I did everything I could to get out of that situation, so they put me back in the rear driving a truck but what they didn't tell me, I was going to be driving ammunition for the infantry units, so I was right back in where I was at. Like I say, I wasn't impressed myself on the training they gave you. They put you in an infantry unit like that without any formal training and that's the reason I feel most of the guys that were casualties in Vietnam was really not trained for the action.

One example, we were on the Cambodian border and we were getting fire in from Cambodia and there wasn't a thing we could do about it but stand there and take it. We wasn't allowed to go in after them or do anything. Another thing that was so sloppy about the war, I thought, that they hired civilian workers that you worked with every day then at night they would go out in the boonies some place and pick up American-made weapons and ammunition that they'd stole from you that day and come back that evening and blow you away with it. I feel that the war was conceived by big corporations and government. I got to know a few of the people when I was there and they really didn't care whether the Americans were there or the North Vietnamese were there. All they were worried about was the meal that day. They heck with tomorrow or next week and that's just about all I have to say about it.

PRESSED FATIGUES

Okay, I'm number fourteen. Before I went to 'Nam I was trained in fire direction patrol. What I did, I sent down commands to the artillery on what setting to put all their guns, to hit what certain target. When I finally got to 'Nam, they gave me two big what they call Radar Chronographs and said, "Here's the book. They're worth $50,00 a piece. Don't break 'em." So from then on, I was more or less kind of on loan. They loaned me out to the ARVN. They loaned me out to the Australians. Anybody that called in would contact the major and say, "Well, we need one of your radar chronographs to check our artillery." Well, they'd say, "Okay, we'll send him out on chopper" and they'd take me out, drop me off somewhere and they'd come back and get me if the Colonel didn't need to go to the PX or something with the chopper. They'd come back out and get me. Then I might be there for two weeks.

Anyhow, when I came back into base camp, I would just kind of drive the major around or something and the biggest thing that I didn't like around there was spit-shine boots and pressed fatigues in the middle of a war zone and after about half the time I was there, we'd be going out on guard duty. We weren't allowed to load our weapon. They'd take the ammunition there with us but you weren't allowed to load. One night, we were out on guard duty and we saw two V.C. come through the first layer of concertina wire. We called back and notified the officer of the day about this so they hashed it around and hashed it around and they said, don't do anything to them. Don't touch them. So they finally walked around a little bit between the two layers of concertina wire and then they went back out the way they came. That's all I got to say.

BOB HOPE SPECIAL

All right, it was 1968, the Bob Hope Special and it came down through the brigade that so many people got to go out of the brigade and so many had to stay at the base camp, so we were about two miles from Duc Long ARVN compound and the C.O., he says half the company could go and half the company could stay and party. They had a party at the company and then the rest of the guys that got to go got to party on the way up and on the way back to Cam Ranh Bay. So the captain put so many names in a hat and we drew names and if you had Bob Hope on it, you got to go and if you had a blank, you had to stay.

So, luckily, I think six out of seven in our squad got to go and the guys that had to stay, well they just went up to Ban Rang and bought out the PX on all the canned beer they had for the party at the camp. So they turned over a jeep trailer and filled it up with ice and beer for the guys at the party and brought down ARVN's to pull perimeter guard while everybody was getting pretty well soused. So, me and about three other guys, we grabbed about eight cases of beer. We wasn't allowed to have the beer. We stuck it in _____, so here we drove 25 miles to Cam Ranh Bay singing Christmas songs and I think it was 125 outside and any decent, self-respecting VC or NVA wouldn't bother us, you know, because they thought we were so crazy and then we get to Cam Ranh Bay finally and like there's already about 20,000 guys there ahead of us so we had to sit a quarter of a mile back from the stage and so everybody was trying to find something to drink and all the PX's and Officer's Clubs and everything were completely sold out for the occasion.

So this one guy from Texas, he was in our squad, he went down and him and another guy they decided to find a bottle, you know, for us to drink while we were sittin' there, and there was M.P.'s all over the place. They were goin' in and out and walking, grabbin' people's booze and stuff. So he went down and he came back a couple of hours later. He finally found a bottle and as soon as he got back to us, I think it took him about two hours to go down and get – to walk back up and down through all the people, and by this time I think there was 30,000 guys there and the M.P.'s was following him all the way back up and he was pretty well shot down so the M.P. got right behind and grabbed his bottle and the guy actually wanted to kill the M.P. and bury him in the sand right there, and so, for taking his bottle after all the trouble that he had gettin' it.

GUNG HO

I did go to Vietnam. At the time I didn't realize there was a political conflict. I figured like a half a million other guys – I was gung ho, so I volunteered to go over from the 339th Engineers in Fort Lewis, Washington, and when I got there – it was a twenty-three hour plane trip and when I landed in Cam Ranh Bay, the pilot and the stewardess and everything, they all disappeared. Nobody could figure out why. So here the sergeant come up and he told us to unload off the plane. So as soon as the first guy jumped off the plane, somebody started shootin'. So they said, "you got to get in all these buses – we're going to take you to the replacement center."

So everybody just started scramblin' and crawlin' for the buses and as soon as they had forty guys in a bus, well they pulled out. I think it took two hours to unload and then we got to the replacement center. So here they were, just sendin' all these guys out here and there and I was just waitin' and waitin' and I was pulled for perimeter guard for a replacement company and my M.O.S. – I was a combat engineer. I think I was there two days and the company I was assigned to sent a truck for me and we stopped at the PX – this was when I first really started realizin' what was going on about Vietnam – the impression I got. So all these guys they started buyin' cases of booze and stuff real cheap. I think it was $1.25 a full quart of Royal Crown Supreme, stuff like that. So the two guys that went to pick us up had loaded up with all this Crown Supreme Royal. I think they had twenty cases of it and me and these – well three other guys and I, replacements, we sat in back and we drove 25 miles and by the time we got there, we were pretty smashed, so we had to stand in front of the brigade colonel and they had to carry me up and stand me up in the ranks to see him and then they finally got me back to bed.

The next day-then we went out and I was assigned to a combat engineer unit building bridge piers – around piers and stuff so they couldn't drop bombs in the river, flow it down to blow things up. They had these pier protectors we built and I don't know what else to say. I seen a lot of action but people, I guess, they liked this, it was good for their economy and everything.

SUPER JOCK

A guy I knew that went to school with, went to Vietnam and got killed. To give you some background on this guy, he was your basic super-jock in high school, but he was a real nerd and he would just hassle people in high school and I don't know about two or three people who liked him and he'd come by and oh, he'd kick other guys in the privates and he really was a pretty tough guy and he was used to being a bully. He went to Vietnam and got killed and whenever they brought his body back and they had the funeral and everything, at the funeral home his dad got all upset and started to tear his uniform off him in the open casket. His dad just started rippin' the buttons off of it and sayin', "I don't want to see that damn uniform" and got all upset. They turned around and put a monument up to this guy in the town where I live and it just seems kind of ironic that they started a fund, a trust fund or scholarship for this guy. It seemed kind of ironic that a real nerd like that, no one likes, that was just, I don't know how to describe this guy – and turn around and do all these nice things and playin' him up like being a super dude and he really wasn't.

SPECTATOR

My involvement in Vietnam was strictly as a spectator. When I turned eighteen the draft had no longer been in effect and all that I learned about Vietnam was either what I heard on the radio, television or read in the newspapers, but the one thing that really got me was how many guys lost their lives and when we pulled out we didn't win a damn thing and there was a lot of guys that got killed that had kids back here and their wives not only lost their husbands for a lost cause, but I think it shamed the country for being in a war like that, because it was just a political thing where the rich man got richer and the poor man got poorer and I just hope we never have another war like that again.

WAR GAMES

I re-upped for the draft – not, re-upped, I volunteered for the draft when I went to Vietnam because I knew I'd be going in a couple of months anyhow and it didn't make any difference – that way I could only go for two years. I guess I went as a sort of patriot, you know, not knowing what it was all about and everything. When I first got there I was scared to death like everybody else but you get over that in about a month or so after you're there a little bit. And I was in the 25th Division – that's north of Saigon up along the Cambodian border and my unit was a reactionary force, for the whole division, so we seen a lot of stuff, you know, lots of battles and that but we'd react to the major ones all over the division.

I tell you that after being over there for a whole year, the point that I want to bring out is it seemed like it was war games all the time. Three times during the one year that I was there, we had three major big battles going on all the time. The enemy would be all over the place. We'd fight for a month or two. We'd be fightin' constantly every day but then we'd push them back over the Cambodian border and back up north and then for another month or so you had like a low period where there wasn't any fighting hardly. You had snipers around and that and we'd go back to base camp and we'd stay there and we didn't do too much maybe. Now, all of a sudden, they'd bring us in and tell us that there's a division right outside of base camp. There's a regiment down next to Saigon. I mean they're all over the place.

Now, with our intelligence and everything what I'd like to know, is how they got there without us knowin' – without us seein' them. I mean, we had planes that took pictures on a night map and you could see them at night. Now, how did these people get back in back over the border? Instead of us holding them out into Cambodia and up north and that, we never held them out. We just let them come back in and then we started fightin' again. For another two months or so you had heavy fightin' and after that you'd go back to the same low period. Now, this happened three times in the one year that I was there and just like a war game to me. Just like, you know, push them out and we'd just ignore them and let them come in and build back up and all of a sudden, there's divisions around us and regiments and back to fightin' again for three months. So to me it was like a big game. The powers, the people, running the war, it was like playing war games.

ALCOHOLICS

I never made it to Vietnam but I joined the Air Force just out of high school and I got moved around quite a bit while I was in there and one of the places I went to was remote and isolated Alaska. It was up above the Arctic Circle and it was – one thing that really – I realize it now but I didn't realize it then, was there was no TV or radio or anything like that up there. Everything centered right around the N.C.O. club and I know from being up there that out of the 100 people that was there, four or five were all boozed up every weekend and every night, you know, even old guys that were almost out of the service. They just turned into alcoholics because they were without their family and everything like that. But I know the first night I got there you had to go through initiation and that was, go to the N.C.O. club and they would mix a great big glass full of everything on the bar. Most people couldn't drink all that the first time, but as time went on, everybody got to be where they could just drink and drink and go throw up and drink some more.

I know everybody does a little bit of drinking in high school, which I did too, but up there was the first time I ever been where I would go to some of the parties or something and not remember anything about it the next day after I woke up. It got to be – I know we got all our beer and booze in once a year on a barge when the river would thaw out and cokes and everything come in at once and just before the barge come in and just before I left, they run out of beer and they had two priority one flights of beer they flew in because morale was sinkin' so low. Even when the chaplain would come there once every month or six weeks, they would even get drunk with you and it was, I don't know, it was an experience to see how a lot of guys react different to something like that.

I saw one guy, he was going to get out of the service as soon as he left there and you see a lot of "Dear John" letters and stuff like that from wives. It's pretty rough on a lot of people. I really think it was a good experience. I wouldn't trade it for anything. It pretty well started me to boozin' pretty heavy, but I guess a place like that helps you grow up a lot.

BELIEVE IT OR NOT

I'll talk a little bit about the black market. Number four. When I first went over there, C-rations were bringing about $45 a case and you could sell them anywhere in Saigon, anywhere in the city, anywhere where they had civilians. Later on, when we started closing up units, things were being sold by individuals such as air conditioners. They were bringing two to five hundred dollars. The same way with a jeep. You could take a jeep in Saigon on Thu Do Street and in a matter of twenty to thirty minutes you could sell that thing for six hundred dollars cash, American money, brand new $50 bills. We were also selling sniper weapons over there. They were bringing two to three hundred dollars and I seen a whole conex sold by an officer, a whole conex full of M-14 sniper weapons with scopes. People over there were making a lot of money off of this. Ice machines was something big in that area, the tents, everything was bringing from two to three to four to five to six hundred. A deuce and a half brought a thousand dollars and these people that had these were selling them. What happened, they would steal them theirselves, take them to the unit, use them and when they got ready to close down, they had an excess of equipment there. Instead of trying to turn it in or get rid of it, they would sell it and the ARVN's would buy it and so would the civilian population over there. Everybody would buy these items. I remember a case, well, the conex of M-14 weapons. I remember them being sold.

Smuggling things back to the States. I was in an aircraft unit and we had to send our tailbooms from the

UH-1 type aircraft back to the States for overhaul when they were shot up. We couldn't destroy them and I know of one individual that put a star light scope in a tailboom of one of these aircraft, sent it back, a friend of his worked in an overhaul unit in Corpus Christi, Texas. Took this scope out and he got the scope when he got back to the States. Now this star light scope is something that I don't think should be in the hands of civilians. Now there is one in the State of Pennsylvania that a young man is using and that is a fine piece of equipment and the only problem is getting batteries. He has to adopt it over to use civilian type batteries.

Drugs – a warrant officer that I know of had a set of speakers. These speakers were two by two by about three and a half feet tall and he shipped that thing, took the speakers out of it, filled these cabinets full of heroin completely to equal out the weight, which were pretty heavy with those seven speakers in each cabinet and sent it back to the States and it went through whole baggage and it was delivered to his house, all of this marijuana. Now a thimble of pure marijuana over there would run you about $10. That's about the size – they call it a vial, about a thimble full. This man brought back pounds upon pounds. He's now living on a big yacht and he's running out of California on this drug selling – drugs that he sent back.

Several cases where people sent stuff back through whole baggage. They just didn't check the speakers. Didn't take the speakers apart. They didn't tear down some of the stereo equipment that was being sent back and more heroin came back that way than anything I know of and I know of many cases. Most of these, believe it or not, were done by warrant officers and aviators and people of this nature that would bring this stuff back. Usually when you would come out of a country, they would spot check two or three people and they was always two or three of them standing around. They knew where to pass these bags of drugs back and forth, who to give them to and that's how they got them out that way. When they called you for a spot check, all you did was hand it to one of your friends there and he held it till you'd go through the spot check and then you went back and picked it up and carried it on the plane and brought it on through.

I was in Aviatio
two years schooling befo
NBC School – Nuclear, Biol
and that, we hear a lot of hu
biological warfare going on and w
these biological weapons, but I was d
that and we didn't use them but we alwa
were always on standby. They were ready
we needed them. Just as fast as we could have
pound bomb and put it on an aircraft, we could h
a 750 pound biological warfare bomb – a CBU b
and put it on that aircraft. A 500 pound bomb might p
hole in the ground about ten feed square. The sam
biological warfare bomb might kill 25,000 people and
ruin two or three square miles of land, but normal people
just don't hear about this and it's really going on.

tely
r, it
this
nbs,
had
was
omb
and
that
the
the

n it.
day.
bout

n Ordinance in the Navy and I had
e I went overseas and I went to
gical and Chemical Warfare,
sh, hush, there's not any
e really don't have all of
irectly involved with
s had them. They
to go any time
taken a 500
ve taken
omb —
t a
e

tour times a day to make sure there was no visible leaks. Aboard carriers, especially the one I was on their magazines have bombs, rockets, missiles and everything. This particular magazine which was by several others, but had its own private elevator. That was the only thing that was used for, was these particular bombs and that was a big waste of money because there was magazines right next to it, five decks below it and every deck down below it. It would have been very easy to use that magazine any time you had to have your conventional weapons up and your other magazine was down but you still couldn't use this special bomb magazine.

MIDDLE OF NOWHERE

I was in Vietnam from July 28, 1971 to July 28, 1972. While I was there, I was an illuminator operator on 130 gunships. The big impression the war had on me was that it was a politician's war. There was fightin' going on all over the place, but nothin' was ever accomplished. It was a war that went on and on and on and kept drawing out and the reason it kept drawin' out was because there was no public pressure at the time. Well, when public pressure started, the politicians started slackin' off on it. We'd fly missions over there that were seemly for no reason at all to have a mission for that. We'd fly areas where there was no V.C. known in the area, and we'd drop flares for F-4's. They'd in and strafe and there wouldn't even be nothin' there. You'd just be out in the middle of nowhere.

We'd be flying along and they'd call us in for a fire mission, like on a fire base, we'd be flyin' perimeter-where the fire bases were bein' constructed. We'd be flyin' perimeter and during the end of the war – well, not toward the end of the war – toward the end of my time there, the last offense was started and while we was flyin' perimeter they'd call us in like I say, for a fire run. We'd go in and fire and we'd run out of ammo. The A.C. would go back when we'd go back to the base and he put in a requisition to find out what happened to the ammunition and here he found out they have a quota of how many rounds you could take out and fire for a particular mission and to me, in a war like that, there's no way in hell that you're goin' to win if you can only shoot twenty bullets a night.

How in the hell are you going to win, if the enemy has two or three thousand bullets and that's the biggest bitch I had about the war. I felt that it was a political war and that it probably would still be going on if wasn't for the public bringing up about people being killed for no reason at all and drawing it out.

NO DECISION

I spent from August 1965 to August 1967 in the Republic of Vietnam and it's my belief that the war itself was political and I'll try to give a few instances where I could see this, and one of the big factors, was for any major decision, we had a Commander-in-Chief, which by then was General Westmoreland, and he was a very competent guy as far as he was allowed to go, which, you know, if there were any major decisions to be made, he could not attack on any place or do anything without first contacting Washington; which for instance, you can see where Cambodia became involved and we wasn't allowed to go into Cambodia after the enemy, even though they would come over to Vietnam and attack the forces and go back, and there's a very good instance over there where, you know, no decision was made.

There were people killed, just because they couldn't get the orders or they couldn't get the bombing raids or whatever it was set up the way it should have been done. It's my belief that when I first went over there, the war itself, I didn't know at the time that it was political, you know. I really thought that I was patriotic, or whatever you call it, but after time went on, you realized that, you know, you don't operate a war sittin' back, you know. And in a sense they decided, you know, or tried to fool people or whatever it was because they would set down the boundary lines of you can't go into Cambodia, or you can't bomb this place or don't bomb this place. When you go to war, you should declare war and let those people know that you're going to do anything that you have to do to win a war, which was never done over there. They told us where we was going to bomb, where you couldn't bomb and like, these people operate all of it and it just become a political war in my opinion.

THE REASONS WHY

I spent from October of '63 until September of '67 in the service. Never spent any time in Vietnam. Not due to the fact that I wouldn't go or wouldn't have went had it come down to that. As far as my views go on the war, I didn't know what the war was about and probably none of us really do and in my opinion, it was a political war and whether it was to be or wasn't to be, I'm not to say, but I'm saying that we had – the United States sent men over there and lost many lives and others that didn't want to go dodged the draft or deserted or went to Canada and this fact really burns me up. To think that we sent our boys over there and they lost their lives maybe for no reason at all and then, like I say, I don't know the reasons why we was over there, but we lost thousands of lives and then these boys went to Canada and other places and deserted and as far as I'm concerned, the United States has no place for them. They shouldn't even recognize them and that's the way I feel about it.

NEVER HURT ANYBODY

I would like to give my viewpoints on the Vietnam war in the way of two situations. One, as a civilian very concerned for a dear friend of mine that was in Vietnam at the time I was still at West Virginia University and number two, I would like to give my viewpoints after I was in the Navy, which I didn't go any time in the Vietnam area, but I was still in the service and earned the proper rights to being awarded by V.A. check for being in the service during the Vietnam war.

But getting back to what I was saying as being a civilian, I had a buddy that was stationed near Saigon and he was detailed to a duty that I felt was really rough. He was what we call perimeter watch and he was given a dog which I guess he had to train himself and this dog supposedly was a trained killer and he'd be put on this perimeter watch, which he might have to watch maybe an area of four to six hundred yards. At the end of this six hundred yards there'd be another man, also the same detail with his dog and he used to write me these letters that in the evening the Vietcong would start the mortar and they'd mortar in and they'd have these Cong that would come in that would have bombs on them like home-made bombs and he said that at certain times they would attack right at you and try to detonate you along with theirselves so I was very concerned with this and I tried to put myself in this position and every time I did, I became very frightened. I'd even shake at times. Really scared about the idea that I was fortunate that I was still in college and not over where he was at.

So one day while I was sitting in health ed class I sat there and I thought, well, things are really getting hairy now and I'm not in the upper third of my class. I may have to go myself, and I kept picturing myself in the situation he was in. So not being cowardly or try to run away to Canada or anything, I went down and took a test for the Navy and two weeks later, I was called back down and told that I could be put on a ninety day delayed program in that after the semester, which ended in December, that I could go ahead and go to the Navy. So I planned on this program and sure enough, three months later I was on my way to the Great Lakes.

So then after being in the service, I also had another close friend that was drafted and this boy had to be a conscientious objector, so he was sent off to Fort Knox, Kentucky for his training even though he was a conscientious objector, he was forced to go. So whenever he got out of boot camp, they sent him to Medical Corpsman school and he kept communicating back and forth with me and this really upset me – a man that is a conscientious objector, they put him in corps school. Why didn't they stick him into an M.O.S. rate that is, you know, like typist or something like this, mail handler. So by and by, six months later he finished A.I.T. in this school and all and they shipped his ass off to Vietnam and all along, I being in the service myself, I thought how corrupt this God-damned government is. It made me more or less hate the United States government and the officials that had the authority to do this to any man.

So, I was stationed to the Patuxy River in 1969 and I was shipped to the Med where I was, I was off the coast of Egypt, whenever the United States had some American citizens aboard planes that were hijacked off the coast of Egypt and about this time, I got a letter from this boy and he was telling me that he was near the demilitarized zone and he was really, you know, in every action as a corpsman and he kept in his letters, he kept telling me, what the hell am I doin' here. He'd never hurt anybody in his life and he didn't even believe in war, but I guess about two or three months there he realized that he would have to defend himself or get killed in the war. So we come back from the Med and I read an article in the paper. I couldn't believe it. It seemed like the same week we got back from the Med and I looked and I read an article about a local boy that was killed in Vietnam and it happened to be this individual I'm speaking of.

So in conclusion, I would like to say that the Vietnam war to me even though I wasn't involved physically, I was involved mentally and it more or less gave me a tendency to hate the United States authorities for some of the shit they pulled on some of the boys that really had to go to Vietnam and then, whenever you think of the men that took the other route and went to Canada, I don't blame them a damn bit.

HELL OF A GUY

I would like to tell another story about the kind of officers and people that ran the war down at the level where I was. I didn't get to see any colonels or anything like that. We had a hell of a good major when I first went over and we were an Air Cav company. We had three helicopters and transport helicopters and scout helicopters and they was red, white and blue. Well, our commanding officer was red, and like I say, he was a hell of a guy. Good pilot and he got in wherever the party was. Well, of course, since he was so good, he made Lieutenant Colonel and went to Tan Sanh Hut. So we got another major to be the commanding officer and instead of being known as "red" he was known as "pink." He was about 5'8", 250 pounds and had been an ROTC graduate from William and Mary College and his first order of business when he got there was to take everybody off the line where we were out working maintenance and plant flowers in front and around his hootch and paint the windows in his hootch and shit like that. A weird hell of a guy. I had to fly with him three or four times and everybody else was down there getting shot at and we're flying at 10,000 feet, approximately, because they didn't have anything that could reach us at 10,000 feet.

GOT MY TIME

I would like to talk about the 1968 Tet Offensive. It was a big blast. They got the safest base at Cam Ranh Bay and where I was, was thirty miles from it and we had -it was New Year's Eve and the guys on guard duty, you know, had arranged for these girls to come down from the village and we had bunkers all around the compound and each girl had her own bunker and they had cots in it and stuff like that. So here I was pretty well soused up and everything and I waited in the line for this one girl. I think for an hour and a half. I think she had something like thirty guys standing outside waitin'....$5.00 a piece and so I got in and got out and got my time and I went back to the club and so I'm leaving the club, and right about 11:55 everyone had planned in the company to have this "mad minute", you know, like at the stroke of midnight they was going to throw all the grenades, shoot all the machine guns, shoot all the flares just for one minute and really raise hell.

I was walking back out of the club, and here was these girls sittin' there countin' their money. So Mamasan, the leader of them was there and another girl was there and I don't know what time it was. It was just a quick reaction, you know. At 12:00 o'clock everything just started goin' off like it had been planned but these girls didn't know about it. So as soon as they heard the machine guns and grenades, right away they turned as white as a ghost. So the only thing I could think of was grab that money and run like hell. So I got about $1000 that night and there wasn't nothing they could do about it. They were there illegally.

138

HOUSE WITH MAIDS

I was stationed in Vietnam from April of '68 to April of '69. I was stationed with the 69th Signal Battalion on Tanh Son Hut Air Base in Saigon and our primary mission was in communications with Military Assistance Command, Vietnam. I wanted to say and tell how the men – the officers of that war ran that war for the men that were out in the field. I was never in the field and I never even carried a rifle while I was over there. As a matter of fact, I only had one in my hand once, but the men who were running that war and living in Saigon were so far removed from that war, that there is no way that they could have ever known what was going on. You had the man in charge – General Abrams – who was living in a two story apartment house with maids and God knows what all he had in that apartment. You had all the Colonels living in villas – abandoned French villas downtown and Lord knows what they had in those villas. There's no way in the world that they could have known what was going on in that war other than hearsay and these men were out there fighting for something that they didn't even know. The men that were running the war didn't know what was going on. That's all I have.

GARBAGE CANS

I was in Vietnam from June of '68 to June of '69 at Chu Lai. It is abut sixty miles south of Da Nang. The thing I remember most about being over there was about being in the army at all. It was just the general ineptitude of the NCO's and some of the career officers. One story I remember a lot about was, well I have two. One was we had a Sergeant that come over with eighteen years in the service and he was an E-5 and in thirteen months I was an E-5. Once he got there he made E-6 and so, he was our shop foreman.

We were an aircraft maintenance company and he come in one day and he said he had a report that Charlie was takin' our scrap metal and makin' home-made bombs out of it, so he wanted us to (indistinguishable)...He was in the sheet metal shop. So we spent two or three hours makin' two great big garbage cans and stippled them, metal and trash, you know, and then the time came for us to clean up the shop and dump the garbage and everything and we asked that guy, well, what do you want us to do with this metal garbage now. Dump it in the bin back with the other garbage. All this time we were makin' two separate garbage cans and then at the end of the day, we dumped them both in the same bins. Because this guy was an E-6, fine. You could tell he had eighteen years in the service.

SOUTH EAST ASIAN ALBUM

The scenes on the following pages are not unique. We offer them to provide a glimpse of the everyday world in which our war was fought.

Several of these photos were smuggled into this country past military censors, often in dirty laundry that got only passing attention from inspectors. Quality and condition varied widely in 1977 and have not improved with age. This edition includes color where available and modern technologies have been used to improve clarity while remaining true to the nature of the originals. All photos are from the 1977 collection but a few changes to the originally published photos have been made to meet spacing limitations.

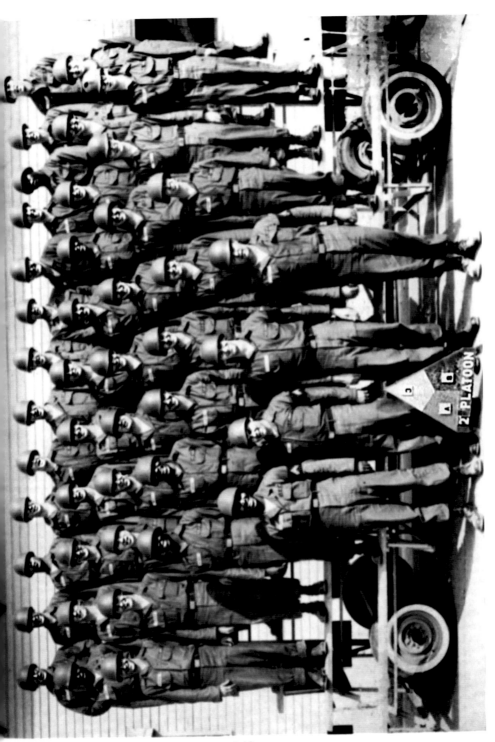

143

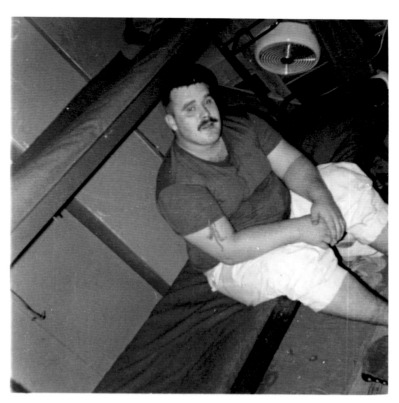

155

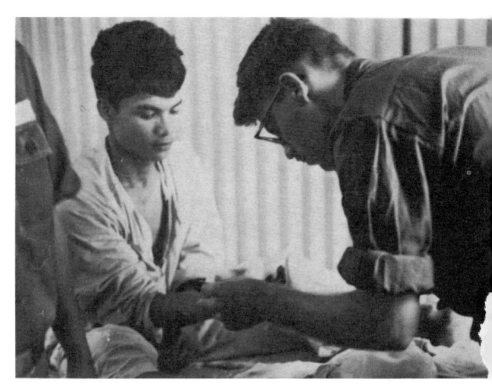

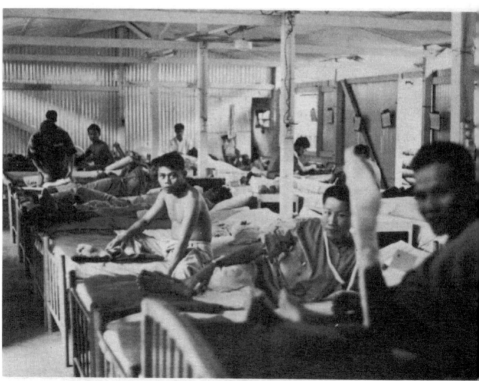

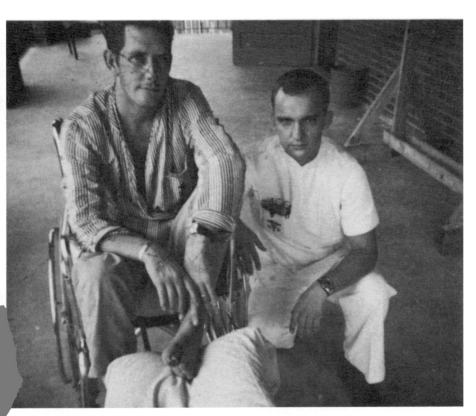

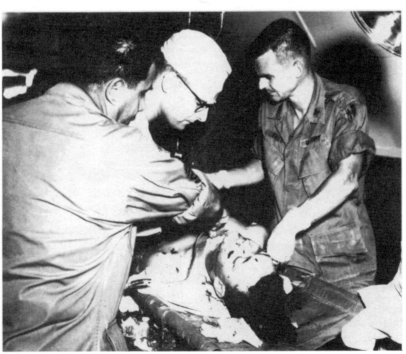